To Mele with best
wishes for a good trip
and a happy year.
   Lovingly
      Helen

WINNOWED WISDOM

WINNOWED WISDOM

WISDOM

A NEW BOOK OF HUMOUR

BY STEPHEN LEACOCK

NEW YORK
DODD, MEAD AND COMPANY
1926

PRINTED IN U. S. A.

THE VAIL-BALLOU PRESS
BINGHAMTON AND NEW YORK

PREFACE

An Appeal to the Average Man

It is the especial aim of this book to make an appeal to the average man. To do this the better, I have made a study of the census of the United States and of the census of Canada, in order to find out who and what the average man is.

In point of residence, it seems only logical to suppose that the average man lives at the centre of population, in other words, in the United States he lives at Honkville, Indiana, and in Canada at Red Hat, Saskatchewan.

In the matter of height the average man is five feet, eight inches, decimal four one seven, and in avoirdupois weight he represents 139 pounds, two ounces, and three pennyweights. Eight-tenths of his head is covered with hair and his whiskers if spread over his face could cover it to *the extent of one-tenth of an inch. This ought to be a promising sign in a reader.*

The average man goes to church six times a year and has attended Sunday school for two afternoons and can sing half a hymn.

Although it thus appears that the average man is rather weak on religion, in point of morals the fellow is decidedly strong. He has spent only one week of his whole life in the penitentiary. Taking an average of theft and dividing it by the population it appears that he has stolen only two dollars and a quarter. And he never tells a lie except where there is some definite material advantage.

The average man is not, by statistics, a great traveller. The poor fellow has been only sixty-two miles away from his own home. He owns nine-tenths of a Ford car, punctures a tire once every twenty-two days, and spends, in the course of his whole life, a month and a half underneath his car.

The education of the average man cost $350. But it didn't get him far. He stopped—according to the educational statistics—within one year of being ready for a college. Most of the things

he learned had no meaning for him.   He gave up
algebra without yet knowing what it was about.

.   .   .   .

By the time I had got to this point of the investigation I began to realize what a poor shrimp
the average man is.   Think of him with his mean
stature and his little chin and his Ford car and his
fear of the dark and his home in Honkville, Indiana, or Red Hat, Saskatchewan.   And think
of his limited little mind!   The average man, it
seems, never forms an opinion for himself.   The
poor nut can't do it.   He just follows the opin-
ions of other men.

I would like ever so much to start a movement
for getting above the average.   Surely if we all
try hard, we can all lift ourselves up high above
the average.   It looks a little difficult mathe-
matically, but that's nothing.

Think how fine it would be to get away from
the average—to mingle with men seven feet high
and women six feet round; to consort with people
who wouldn't tell a lie except for big money, and
to have friends who could solve cross-word puzzles without having to buy the Encyclopaedia
Britannica!

But the only trouble with such a movement is that if I did really start it, and if I could, with great labor and persuasion, get it going and it began to succeed, then who would come flocking into it but the darned little average man himself. As long as it was unsuccessful, he'd keep out of it. But let it once succeed and in he'd come. That's exactly his dirty little nature.

In short, now that I think of it I am not so keen on appealing to the average man. Nothing ever does appeal to him, until it has made a terrible hit somewhere else.

. . . .

I had just brought my investigation to this point when I realized that I had forgotten all about the average woman. What about her? Where does she come out?

So I picked up the census volumes again and took another little run through them.

The average woman, it seems, does not live at Honkville, Indiana, or at Red Hat, Saskatchewan. The percentage of women in the population being much greater in the eastern part of the country, the average woman lives one hundred and five miles east of the average man. But she is getting *nearer to him every day. Oh, yes, she is after him, all right!*

It is also clear that the average woman is about half an inch taller than the average man. Women, taken individually, are no doubt not so tall as men, but, on the average, a woman is just a little taller. Men will find it a little difficult to understand how this can be, but any woman can see it at once.

In point of personal appearance, it may be estimated that women, taken as an average, wear their hair just below their shirt collar and have their skirts, at an average, always two inches higher than they were a year before.

The average woman gets married at twenty-seven, has two children and a quarter, and is divorced once in every eight years.

In morals the average woman is away ahead of the man. Everybody knows this in a general way, but it is very pleasing to see it corroborated by cold, hard statistics.

The man as we have seen above, spends a week in the penitentiary. But the woman is there only half a day. In her whole life she consumes only one and a half gills of whiskey, but, on the other hand, she eats, according to the director of the census, four tons of candy. She is devoted to her two and a quarter children, but she makes more fuss over the quarter of a child than she does over the two whole ones.

In point of intellect, the average woman cannot reason and cannot think. But she can argue. The average woman, according to the educational section of the census, only got as far in arithmetic as improper fractions. Those stopped her.

And yet, take her as she is—even with her hair bobbed round her ears and her skirt higher than it was, and her inability to add or to reason—she is all right. The average man comes out of the investigation as a poor insignificant shrimp. But with the average woman, the more you think about her, the better she appears.

Perhaps on second thoughts I might dedicate this book to the average woman. But then, unfortunately, the average woman reads nothing, —or nothing except love stories.

STEPHEN LEACOCK

McGill University
1926

Contents

Contents

I
THE OUTLINES OF EVERYTHING

The Outlines of Everything

Designed for Busy People at Their Busiest

A Preface to the Outlines

WITHIN recent years it is becoming clear that a university is now a superfluous institution. College teaching is being replaced by such excellent little manuals as the "Fireside University Series," the "World's Tiniest Books," the "Boys Own Conic Sections," and the "Little Folks Spherical Trigonometry." Thanks to books such as these no young man in any station of life need suffer from an unsatisfied desire for learning. He can get rid of it in a day. In the same way any business man who wishes to follow the main currents of history, philosophy and radio-activity may do so while changing his shirt for dinner.

The world's knowledge is thus reduced to a

3

very short compass. But I doubt if even now it is sufficiently concentrated. Even the briefest outlines yet produced are too long for the modern business man. We have to remember that the man is busy. And when not busy he is tired. He has no time to go wading through five whole pages of print just to find out when Greece rose and fell. It has got to fall quicker than that if it wants to reach him. As to reading up a long account, with diagrams, of how the protozoa differentiated itself during the twenty million years of the pleistocene era into the first invertebrate, the thing is out of the question. The man hasn't got twenty million years. The whole process is too long. We need something shorter, snappier, something that brings more immediate results.

From this point of view I have prepared a set of Outlines of Everything covering the whole field of science and literature. Each section is so written as to give to the busy man *enough* and just exactly enough of each of the higher branches of learning. At the moment when he has had enough, I stop. The reader can judge for himself with what accuracy the point of complete satiety has been calculated.

4

Volume One—The Outline of
Shakespeare

[*Designed to make Research Students in Fifteen Minutes. A Ph.D. degree granted immediately after reading it.*]

1. *Life of Shakespeare.* We do not know when Shaksper was born nor where he was born. But he is dead.

From internal evidence taken off his works after his death we know that he followed for a time the profession of a lawyer, a sailor and a scrivener and he was also an actor, a bartender and an ostler. His wide experience of men and manners was probably gained while a bartender. (Compare. Henry V. Act V. Scene 2, "Say now, *gentlemen, what shall yours be?*")

But the technical knowledge which is evident upon every page shows also the intellectual training of a lawyer. (Compare. Macbeth. Act VI. Scene 4. *"What is there in it for me?"*) At the same time we are reminded by many passages of Shakspere's intimate knowledge of the sea. (Romeo and Juliet. Act VIII, Scene 14. *"How is her head now, nurse?"*)

We know, from his use of English, that Shag-sper had no college education.

HIS PROBABLE PROBABILITIES

As an actor Shicksper, according to the current legend, was of no great talent. He is said to have acted the part of the ghost and he also prob-ably took such parts as *Enter a citizen, a Tucket sounds, a Dog barks, or a Bell is heard within.* (Note. We ourselves also have been a Tucket, a Bell, a Dog and so forth in our college dramatic days. Ed.)

In regard to the personality of Shakespere, or what we might call in the language of the day Shakespere the Man, we cannot do better than to quote the following excellent analysis done, we think, by Professor Gilbert Murray, though we believe that Brander Matthews helped him a lit-tle on the side.

"Shakespere was probably a genial man who probably liked his friends and probably spent a good deal of time in probable social intercourse. He was probably good tempered and easy going with very likely a bad temper. We know that he

6

drank (Compare. Titus Andronicus. Act I, Scene I. *"What is there to drink?"*), but most likely not to excess. (Compare. King Lear. Act II. Scene I. *"Stop!"* and see also Macbeth. Act X. Scene 20. *"Hold! Enough!"*) Shakespere was probably fond of children and most likely of dogs, but we don't know how he stood on porcupines.

"We imagine Shakespeare sitting among his cronies in Mitre Tavern, joining in the chorus of their probable songs, and draining a probable glass of ale, or at times falling into reverie in which the majestic pageant of Julius Caesar passes across his brooding mind."

To this excellent analysis we will only add. We can also imagine him sitting any where else we like—that in fact is the chief charm of Shakesperian criticism.

The one certain thing which we know about Shakespere is that in his will he left his second best bed to his wife.

Since the death of S. his native town—either Stratford upon Avon or somewhere else—has become a hallowed spot for the educated tourist. It is strange to stand today in the quiet street of the little town and to think that here Shakespeare actually lived—either here or elsewhere—and that England's noblest bard once mused among these willows—or others.

WORKS OF SHAKESPEARE

Our first mention must be of the Sonnets, written probably, according to Professor Matthews, during Shakesbur's life and not after his death. There is a haunting beauty about these sonnets which prevents us from remembering what they are about. But for the busy man of today it is enough to mention, *Drink to me only with thine eyes, Rock Me to Sleep Mother, Hark, Hark, the Dogs do Bark.* Oh, yes, quite enough. It will get past him every time.

The Historical Plays

Among the greatest of Shakespeare's achievements are his historical plays,—Henry I, Henry II, Henry III, Henry IV, Henry V, Henry VI, Henry VII and Henry VIII. It is thought that Shakespeare was engaged on a play dealing with

8

Henry IX when he died. It is said to have been his opinion that having struck a good thing he had better stay with it.

There is doubt as to authorship of part, or all, of some of these historical plays. In the case of Henry V, for example, it is held by the best critics that the opening scene (100 lines) was done by Ben Jonson. Then Shakespeare wrote 200 lines (all but half a line in the middle) which undoubtedly is Marlowe's.

Then Jonson, with a little help from Fletcher, wrote 100 lines. After that Shakespear, Massinger and Marlowe put in 10 lines each. But from this point the authorship is confused, each sticking in what he could.

But we ourselves are under no misapprehension as to what is Shakespeare's and what is not. There is a touch which we recognize every time. When we see the real Shakespeare, we know it. Thus, whenever it says *"A Tucket Sounds. Enter Gloucester with Hoboes,"* we know that Shakespeare, and only Shakespeare, could have thought of that. In fact Shakespeare could bring in things that were all his own, such as:—*"Enter Cambridge followed by An Axe." "Enter Ox-*

ford followed by a Link." His lesser collaborators could never get the same niceness of touch. Thus, when we read, "Enter the Earl of Richmond followed by a pup," we realize that it is poor work.

Another way in which we are able to test whether or not a historical play is from Shakespeare's own pen is by the mode of address used by the characters. They are made to call one another by place designations instead of by their real names. "What says our brother France?" or "Well, Belgium, how looks it to you?" "Speak on, good Burgundy, our ears are yours." We ourselves have tried to imitate this but could never quite get it; our attempt to call our friends "Apartment B, the Grosvenor," and to say "Go to it, the Marlborough, Top Floor No. 6" has practically ended in failure.

THE GREAT TRAGEDIES

Every educated person should carry in his mind an outline idea of the greatest of Shakespeare's tragedies. This outline when reduced to what is actually remembered by playgoers and students is not difficult to acquire. Sample:

HAMLET (not to be confused with *Omelette* which was written by Voltaire). Hamlet, Prince of Denmark, lived among priceless scenery and was all dressed in black velvet. He was deeply melancholy. Either because he was mad, or because he was not, Hamlet killed his uncle and destroyed various other people whose names one does not recall.

The shock of this drove Ophelia to drown herself, but oddly enough when she threw herself in the water she floated, and went down the river singing and shouting. In the end Hamlet killed Laertes and himself, and others leaped into his grave until it was quite full when the play ends. People who possess this accurate recollection rightly consider themselves superior to others.

SHAKESPEARE AND COMPARATIVE LITERATURE

Modern scholarship has added greatly to the interest in Shakespeare's work by investigating the sources from which he took his plays. It appears that in practically all cases they were old stuff already. Hamlet quite evidently can be traced to an old Babylonian play called *HUM-LID* and this itself is perhaps only a version of a Hindoo tragedy, *The Life of William Johnson.*

The play of Lear was very likely taken by S. from the old Chinese drama of *Li-Po,* while Macbeth, under the skilled investigation of modern scholars, shows distinct traces of a Scottish origin.

In effect, Shakespeare, instead of sitting down and making up a play out of his head, appears to have rummaged among sagas, myths, legends, archives and folk lore, much of which must have taken him years to find.

PERSONAL APPEARANCE

In person Shakespeare is generally represented as having a pointed beard and bobbed hair, with a bald forehead, large wide eyes, a salient nose, a retreating chin and a general expression of vacuity, verging on imbecility.

SUMMARY

The following characteristics of Shakespeare's work should be memorized—majesty, sublimity, grace, harmony, altitude, also scope, range, reach, together with grasp, comprehension, force and light, heat and power.

Conclusion: Shakespeare was a very good writer.

VOLUME TWO—THE OUTLINE OF EVOLUTION

[*Specially Revised to Suit Everybody, and Particularly Adapted for the Schools of Tennessee.*]

IT seems that recently there has been a lot of new trouble about the theory of evolution in the schools. Either the theory is being taught all wrong or else there is something the matter with it. For years it had seemed as if the doctrine of Evolution was so universally accepted as to lose all its charm. It was running as a close second to Spherical Trigonometry and Comparative Religion and there was no more excitement about it than there is over Anthropology.

Then suddenly something seems to have happened. A boy in a Kansas public school threw down his book and said that the next time he was called a protozoon he'd quit the class. A parent in Ostaboola, Oklahoma, wrote to the local school board to say that for anyone to teach his children that they were descended from monkeys cast a doubt upon himself which he found intolerable. After that the wave of protest swept through the colleges.

The students marched in processions carrying banners with the motto "Are we baboons? Rah, Rah, Apes!" The Rotary Clubs of town after town voted by a standing vote that they were unable to support (or to understand) the doctrine of biological biogenesis, and they wanted it taken away.

The Woman's Culture Club of Winona, Utah, moved that the name of Charles Darwin be changed in the text books of the state to that of W. J. Bryan. The Anti-Saloon League voted that the amount of Darwinianism that should be licensed in the schools should not be more than one-half of one per cent.

It is to meet this difficult situation that the present outline of Evolution has been prepared. It is intended so to revise and modify the rigid character of the theory as to make it acceptable to everybody.

The obvious beginning of the matter is to present the theory of evolution as it stood before the trouble began in Tennessee. Each of us at that time carried in his head an outline, a little bit hazy, but still usable, of the Doctrine of Evolution as we remembered it from our college training.

OUTLINE OF EVOLUTION AS DIMLY RECALLED
FROM COLLEGE EDUCATION

We are all descended from monkeys. This descent, however, took place a long time ago and there is no shame in it now. It happened two or three thousand years ago and must have been after and not before the Trojan war.

We have to remember also that there are

15

several kinds of monkeys. There is the ordinary monkey seen in the street with the hand organ (*communis monacus*), the baboon, the giboon (not Edward,) the bright, merry, little chimpanzee, and the hairy ourang-outang with the long arms. Ours is probably the hairy ourang-outang.

But the monkey business is only part of it. At an earlier stage men were not even that. They probably began as worms. From that they worked up to being oysters; after that they were fish, then snakes, then birds, then flying squirrels, and at last monkeys.

The same kind of change passed over all the animals. All the animals are descended from one another. The horse is really a bird, and is the same animal as the crow. The differences between them are purely superficial. If a crow had two more feet and no feathers it would be a horse except for its size.

The whole of these changes were brought about by what is called the Survival of the Fittest. The crookedest snake outlived the others. Each creature had to adapt itself or bust.

The giraffe lengthened its neck. The stork went in for long legs. The hedgehog developed prickles. The skunk struck out an independent line of its own. Hence the animals that we see about us—as the skunk, the toad, the octopus, and the canary—are a highly selected lot.

This wonderful theory was discovered by Charles Darwin. After a five-year voyage in the *Beagle* as a naturalist in the Southern Seas, Darwin returned to England and wrote a book called "Sartor Resartus" which definitely established the descent of mankind from the avoirdupois apes.

One must admit that in this form the theory does not seem calculated to give any great offense to anybody. One must therefore suppose that the whole of the present bitter controversy arose out of what Darwin himself must have written. But this is obviously not so. I have not actually before me the text of Darwin's own writings, but I recall the general run of what he wrote with sufficient accuracy to reproduce it here.

DARWIN'S OWN STATEMENT

[*Personal Recollection of the Work of the Great Naturalist*]

"On the Antilles the common crow, or decapod, has two feet while in the Galapagos Islands it has a third. This third foot, however, does not appear to be used for locomotion, but merely for conversation. Dr. Anderson of H. M. S. *Unspeakable* during his visit to the Galapagos Islands in 1834 saw two crows sitting on a tree. One was, apparently, larger than the other. Dr. Anderson also saw a lizard at Guayaquil in Ecuador which had lost one toe. In fact, he had quite a good time.

"It would be too much to say that the crow and the lizard are the same bird. But there seems little doubt that the apex cervicus of the lizard is of the same structure as the rudimentary dorsal fin of the crow. I put forward this statement however with the modesty which it deserves and am only led to it with deep reluctance and with a full sense of its fatal character.

"I may say that I myself while off the Oesophagus Islands in H. M. S. *Impossible* in the year 1835 saw a flock of birds of the kind called by the sailors "bum-birds," which alighted on the masts and held on by their feet. In fact, I saw a lot of interesting things like that.

"While I was in the *Beagle,* I recall that on one occasion we landed on the Marquesas Islands where our captain and his party were entertained by the chief on hams and yams. After the feast a group of native women performed a hula-hula dance during which I wandered out into the woods and secured a fine collection of toads.

"On the next island—while the captain and his officers were watching a hitchi-kitchi dance—I picked up some admirable specimens of lizards and was fortunate enough to bring back a pocketful of potato bugs."

After reading this plain account as quoted, or at least as remembered, direct from Darwin, one must admit that there is no reason to try to rob him of his discoveries.

But to make the case still plainer, let us set alongside of this a clear simple statement of the Theory of Evolution as it is now held by the

scientists in our colleges. I have before me the
enunciation of the doctrine as stated at the request of the press by a distinguished biologist
during the height of the present controversy.
What he says runs, as follows—or very nearly as
follows:

"All controversy apart, we must at least admit
the existence of a continuous morphological pro-
toplasmic differentiation——"

That seems to me a fair, manly statement of a
plain fact.

"Cytology is still in its infancy—"

This is too bad, but it will grow.

"But at least it involves the admission of a
primitive conformity which removes any priori
difficulty in the way of evolution."

So there we are. After that one would think
that the Tennessee schools would have no further
difficulty about the thing.

THE TIME OF EVOLUTION

But even if we reach a definite conclusion as
to the nature of the process by which life gradually appeared and assumed higher and higher

forms, the question still remains—over how great a period did the process last? What time element must be interposed? In other words as Henri Bergson once stated it with a characteristic flash of genius, "How long did it take?"

The earlier estimates of evolutionary scientists placed the age of man at about 500,000 years. This was ridiculously low. You can't evolve any kind of real man in that time. Huxley boldly raised the figures to 1,000,000. Lord Kelvin, amid unusual applause, put it up to 2,000,000 years. The cheers had hardly died away when Sir Ray Lankester disturbed the whole universe by declaring that man was 4,000,000 years old. Two years later a professor of the Smithsonian Institute raised it to 5,000,000. This estimate was seen and raised to 10,000,000 years. This again was raised from year to year amid universal enthusiasm.

The latest advices are that a student in Schenectady Technical High School places the age of man at 100,000,000 years. For a rough working estimate, therefore, the business man will not be far wrong in assuming (for practical pur-

poses) that the age of man is anything from
100,000,000 to 1,000,000,000. Night watch-
men are perhaps a little older.

POSTSCRIPT: UP TO DATE CORRECTIONS OF THE DARWINIAN THEORY

A still more cheerful light is thrown on the
evolution controversy by the fact that modern
biologists do not entirely hold with the theory
of Charles Darwin. I find on inquiry that they
are prepared to amend his evolution doctrine in
a variety of points.

It seems that Darwin laid too much stress on
what he called natural selection and the survival
of the fittest. The modern biologist attaches no
importance to either of these. It seems also that
Darwin overestimated very much the part played
by heredity. He was moreover mistaken in his
idea of the changes of the species. It is probable, too, that his notion of a monkey is inadequate. It is doubtful also whether Darwin ever
actually sailed on the *Beagle*. He may have
been in the *Phineas Q. Fletcher* of Duluth.
Nor is it certain that his name was Darwin.

VOLUME THREE—THE BUSINESS OUTLINE OF
ASTRONOMY

The world or universe in which we do our business consists of an infinite number, perhaps a hundred billion, perhaps not, of blazing stars accompanied by comets, dark planets, asteroids, asterisks, meteors, meteorites and dust clouds whirling in vast circles in all directions and at all velocities. How many of these bodies are habitable and fit for business we do not know.

The light emitted from these stars comes from distances so vast that most of it is not here yet. But owing to the great distance involved the light from the stars is of no commercial value. One has only to stand and look up at the sky on a clear starlight night to realize that the stars are of no use.

Practically all our efficient light, heat and power comes from the sun. Small though the sun is, it gives out an intense heat. The business man may form some idea of its intensity by imagining the entire lighting system of any two great American cities grouped into a single bulb; it would be but little superior to the sun.

The earth revolves around the sun and at the same time revolves on its own axis, the period of its revolution and the rising and setting of the sun being regulated at Washington, D. C. Some years ago the United States government decided to make time uniform and adopted the system of standard time; an agitation is now on foot,—in Tennessee,—for the lengthening of the year.

The moon, situated quite close to the earth but of no value, revolves around the earth and can be distinctly seen on a clear night outside the city limits. During a temporary breakdown of the lighting plant in New York city a few years ago the moon was quite plainly seen moving past the tower of the Metropolitan Life building. It cleared the Flatiron building by a narrow margin. Those who saw it reported it as somewhat round but not well shaped, and emitting an inferior light which showed that it was probably out of order.

The planets, like the earth, move around the sun. Some of them are so far away as to be of no consequence and, like the stars, may be dismissed. But one or two are so close to the earth that they may turn out to be fit for business. The planet Mars is of especial interest inasmuch as

24

its surface shows traces of what are evidently canals which come together at junction points where there must be hotels. It has been frequently proposed to interest enough capital to signal to Mars, and it is ingeniously suggested that the signals should be *sent in six languages.*

VOLUME FOUR—OUTLINE OF RECENT ADVANCES IN SCIENCE

[*Specially Designed for Members of Women's Culture Clubs, and Representing Exactly the Quantity of Information Carried Away From Lectures on Scientific Progress*]

Einstein's Theory of Relativity. Einstein himself is not what one would call a handsome man. When seen by members of the Fortnightly Women's Scientific Society in Boston he was pronounced by many of them to be quite insignificant in appearance. Some thought, however, that he had a certain air of distinction, something which they found it hard to explain but which they *felt.* It is certain that Einstein knows nothing of dress. His clothes appear as if taken out of the rag bag, and it is reported by two ladies who heard him speak at the University of Pennsylvania on the measurement of rays of light that he wore an absolutely atrocious red tie. It is declared to be a matter of wonder that no one has ever told him; and it is suggested that some one ought to take hold of him.

Einstein is not married. It has been reported, by members of the Trenton (New Jersey) Five O'clock Astronomical Investigation Club that there is a romance in his life. He is thought to have been thrown over by a girl who had a lot of money when he was a poor student, and it was this that turned his mind to physics. It is held that things work that way. Whether married or not he certainly behaved himself like a perfect gentleman at all the clubs where he spoke. He drinks nothing but black coffee.

Einstein's theories seem to have made a great stir.

———

Madame Curie's Discoveries in Radio-Activity. Madame Curie may be a great scientist but it is doubted whether she is a likeable woman or a

woman who could make a home. Two members
of the Omaha Woman's Astronomical and Physical Afternoon Tea Society heard her when she
spoke in Washington on the Radiation of Gamma
Particles from Helium. They say that they had
some difficulty in following her. They say she
was wearing just a plain coat and skirt but had
quite a good French blouse which certainly had
style to it. But they think that she lacks charm.

Rutherford's Researches in the Atomic Theory.
Ernest Rutherford, or rather Sir Ernest Rutherford as it is right to call him because he was
made a knight a few years ago for something he
did with molecules, is a strikingly handsome man
in early middle age. Some people might consider him as beginning to get old but that depends on the point of view. If you consider a
man of fifty an old man then Sir Ernest is old.
But the assertion is made by many members of
various societies that in their opinion a man is
at his *best* at fifty. Members who take that
point of view would be interested in Rutherford.
He has eyes of just that pale steely blue which

suggest to members something powerful and strong, though members are unable to name it. Certainly he made a perfectly wonderful impression on The Ladies Chemico-Physical Research and Amusement Society in Toronto, when he was there with that large British body.

Members of clubs meeting Sir Ernest should remember that he won the Nobel Prize and that it is not awarded for character but is spelled differently.

II
BROTHERLY LOVE
AMONG THE NATIONS

The Next War

FROM everything which I read in the press, I feel certain that it is coming. There doesn't seem the slightest doubt about it. It may not come for a month and it might be a year in coming, but there is no doubt the Next War is already looming in sight.

I have gathered together all the documents that prove it—interviews and discussions with the leading men concerned in it, who simply must know what they are talking about. Let me lay some of them before the reader and he can see for himself, on the very best authority, the situation that confronts us:

DOCUMENT NO. I

The Alignment in the Next War

NEW YORK, July 25.—Colonel The Honourable Fizzle Bangspark of the British General

Army Staff, who arrived yesterday in New York on the *Megalomania,* expressed his views to the representatives of the press on the prospects of the Next War. The Colonel is confident that in the Next War, which he thinks may begin at any time, it is most likely the alignment will be that of Great Britain, France, and the United States against Germany and Russia.

But he may think it equally likely that it may be fought as between Great Britain, Russia, and Germany against France, the United States, and Portugal. Colonel Bangspark states, however, that though the war is certain the exact alignment of the nations will be very difficult to foresee.

He thinks it possible that England and Switzerland, if they get a good opportunity, may unite against France and Scotland. But it is altogether likely that in a war of magnitude, such as Colonel Bangspark hopes to see, the United States and China will insist on coming in, either on one side or the other. "If they do," continued Colonel Bangspark, "it will be hard to keep them out."

32

The distinguished officer considers it difficult to say what part Japan will play in the Next War, but he is sure that it will get into it somewhere. When asked about the part that would be played by the races of Africa in the coming conflict, Colonel Bangspark expressed a certain amount of doubt. "It is hard to say," he stated, "whether they can get in in time. They number of course a great many millions, but the question really turns on whether they have had a training sufficient to let them in. As yet their armies would be hardly destructive enough, and it would be very poor policy to let them in if they do not turn out to be deadly enough when they get in.

"The black," said the colonel, "is a good fellow and I like him. If he were put under first class European officers, he might prove fairly murderous. But I am not as yet prepared to say that we can make a profitable use of him in the Next War."

Asked if the Chinese would play a large part in the coming struggle, the distinguished officer again hesitated. "The Chinaman," he claims, "has not yet had enough contact with European civilizations. The Chinaman is by nature a pacifist and it will be hard to get him away from the idea of peace."

Asked finally if the South Sea Islanders would be in the struggle, Colonel Bangspark spoke warmly and emphatically in their favor. "They will be in it from the start," he said. "I know the Polynesians well, having helped to organize native troops in the Marquesas Islands where I was quartered at Popo Popo for two years, and in the Friendly Islands and in the Society Islands and in the Paradise Group, where I was the first man to introduce gunpowder.

"The Marquesas Islander," the colonel went on, "is a splendid fellow. In many ways he is ahead of us Europeans. His work with the blow-pipe and the poison dart antedates the use of poison in European warfare and compares favorably with the best work of our scientific colleges."

When questioned as to which side the Marquesas Islanders would come in on, the colonel stated that he did not regard that as a matter of prime importance. He was convinced, however, that a place would be found for them and he

34

hoped to see them in the front trenches (on one side or the other) on the first day.

Colonel Bangspark expressed himself as delighted with all that he has seen on this side of the water. He says that he was immensely pleased with the powder works on the Hudson, and though he had not yet seen the powder works on the Potomac, he was convinced that they were just as delightful.

The colonel, whose sojourn in our country is to last for some weeks, will shortly leave New York to visit the powder works at South Chicago. He is accompanied on his journey by his wife and little daughter, both of whom he expects will be blown up in the Next War.

DOCUMENT NO. 2

The Peril From The Air

NEW YORK, July 25.—General de Rochambeau-Lafayette, Director-in-Chief of the French Aerial forces, was interviewed yesterday at the Ritzmore Hotel as to the prospects of world peace. The General, whose full name is the Marquis de Rochambeau-Lafayette de Liancourt

35

de la Rochefoucauld, belongs to the old noblesse of France, and is a cultivated French gentleman of the old school. He is himself a veteran of seven wars and is decorated with the *croix militaire, the croix de guerre,* the *nom de plume,* and the *cri de Paris.*

The Next War will, the count thinks, be opened, if not preceded, by the bombing of New York from the air. The hotels, which the count considers comfortable and luxurious above anything in Europe, will probably be blown up on the first day. The Metropolitan Museum of Art which General de Rochambeau visited yesterday and which he regards as equal to anything in the south of France, would undoubtedly afford an admirable target for a bomb.

The general expressed his unbounded astonishment at the size and beauty of the Pennsylvania and the Grand Central stations. Both, he said, would be blown up immediately. No air squadron could afford to neglect them.

"And your great mercantile houses," the count continued enthusiastically, "are admirable. Combining as they do, a wide superficies with an outline sufficiently *a pic* to make it an excellent *point de mire,* they could undoubtedly be lifted into the air at one bombing."

The Coming Conflict On The Sea

NEW YORK, July 25.—Admirable Breezy, who represents the jolliest type of the hearty British sailor and who makes a delightful impression everywhere, is of the opinion that the Next War will be fought not only on land but on the sea and in the sky and also under the sea.

"It will be fought all over the shop," said the Admirable, "but I do trust that the navy will have its fair share." The big battleship, he says, is after all the great arm of defense. "We are carrying guns now forty feet long and with an effective range of twenty-five miles." "Give me a gun ten feet longer," said the Admirable, "and I will stand off New York and knock down your bally city for you."

He offered further, if given a gun sixty feet long, to reach Philadelphia, and that if he were given the right gun platform he could perhaps hit Pittsburgh.

"I don't despair even of Chicago," said the Admirable. "We are moving forward in naval gunnery every year. It is merely a matter of size, length, and range. I could almost promise you that in ten years I could have a smack at St. Louis and Omaha. Canada, unfortunately, will mostly be on our side; otherwise, one might have had a bang at Winnipeg."

Admirable Breezy said that while he was warmly in favor of peace, he felt that a sea war between England and the United States would certainly make for good fellowship and mutual understanding between the two navies. "We don't know one another," he complained, "and under present circumstances I don't see how we can. But if our fellows could have a smack at your fellows and your fellows have a smack at our fellows, it would make for a good understanding all round."

The Admiral is to speak in Carnegie Hall tonight on *What England Owes to the United States*. A large attendance (of financial men) is expected.

DOCUMENT NO. 4

The New Chemical Terror

New York, July 26.—Professor Gottlos Schwefeldampf, the distinguished German chemist, who is at the head of the German Kriegschemiefabrik at Stinken in Bavaria, arrived in New York yesterday on the *Hydrophobia* and is at the Belmore Hotel. The professor who is a man somewhat below middle stature, is extremely short-sighted, and is at present confined to his room from the effects of a fall down the elevator. He speaks with the greatest optimism on the prospects of chemical warfare.

He considers that it has a wonderful future before it. "In the last war," he declared, sitting up in bed as much as a rheumatic infliction of long standing enabled him to do, "we were only beginning. We have developed now a gas which will easily obliterate the population of a whole town. It is a gas which is particularly destructive in the case of children, but which gives also very promising results with adults."

The professor spoke to the members of the press of the efficiency of this new discovery.

Half a pint of the gas let loose in the room, he said, would easily have annihilated the eight representatives of the press who were present with him. He regretted that unfortunately he had none of the gas in a condition for instant use.

"But we shall not rely alone on gas," continued Professor Schwefeldampf. "In the Next War we expect to make a generous use of poison. Our poison factories are developing methods whereby we can poison the crops in the ground a hundred miles away. If our present efforts reach a happy conclusion, we shall be able to poison the livestock of an entire country. I need not dilate," he said, "on the favorable results of this"——

The Professor was interrupted by a violent fit of coughing, after which he sank back so exhausted that the members of the press were unable to prod any more copy out of him and left.

.   .   .   .

There! That's about the picture, not a bit exaggerated, of where we are letting this poor old world drift to. Can we manage, my dear people, to do something to stir up a little brotherly love all round? We ought to do it even if we have to send hundreds of people to jail to get it. As for me, I intend to start towards it right away. The very next time I see on the street a Russian Bolshevik with black whiskers like an eclipse of the sun, I shall go right up to him and kiss him and say, "Come, Clarence, let us forget the past and begin again."

INTERNATIONAL AMENITIES

Can We Wonder That It's Hard To Keep Friends?

I have been much impressed lately by the way in which the habit of *"scathing denunciation,"* back and forward across the Atlantic, is growing in the press. Every time when international news gets a little slack somebody lands off a steamer and says something about British Education or about American women that sets the whole press into a flame. The people who say the things are of no possible importance. They are for the most part people of whom nobody ever heard before and never will again. But that doesn't matter. The newly arrived visitor stands up on the deck of his steamer, gets the reporters all grouped around him in a ring and then begins to "denounce." As a result next morning the newspapers of the entire continent carry news items such as the following, and the public seethes with indignation.

DENOUNCES AMERICAN EDUCATION

New York, April——

"Mr. Farquhar McSquirt, who holds a high position in the Kindergarten Department of the Scottish Orphans Asylums at Dumfoolish, landed yesterday from the *Aquitania* on a tour of inspection of the American and Canadian schools and at once uttered a scathing denunciation of education on this continent. He considers that the whole educational system of America is punk. He admits that a great many pupils attend school on this continent but denies that they learn a thing. He considers that the average boy of twelve in the Orkney Islands knows more than a graduate of Harvard and Yale. The American student, he says, has never learned to *think;* whereas the

42

Scottish boy begins to think very soon after he learns to talk. Mr. McSquirt considers that the principal cause of the defect of American education is the utter lack of qualified teachers. He claims that the average American school teacher is a complete nut. Few of them stay more than ten years in the profession whereas in Scotland the average period is well over fifty years."

As soon as this kind of thing has been spilt all over the map of North America, the next thing to do is to mop it up. The newspapers send out enquiries to ten heads of ten great universities, and they all answer that while they have not the pleasure of knowing Mr. McSquirt personally,—which means that they hope they never will know him,—they emphatically deny his strictures on our education. They claim that the average American boy, while he may not have such long ears as a Scotch boy, is more receptive. He may not know as much as a Scottish student but what he knows he has digested, a thing the Scottish student has little chance to do. After this the public is soothed and the affair dies down.

Of course it must not be supposed that these "denunciations" are all in one direction. I don't mean for a moment that they are always directed against this continent. Not at all. That merely depends on which direction the traveller is going in. If he is headed the other way and is standing on British soil the denunciation is turned around and it runs something after this fashion.

DENOUNCES OXFORD

London, April——

"Mr. Phineas Q. Cactus, T.Q., P.F., Principal of the Texas Normal Institute for Feeble Minded Navajo Indians, has just attracted wide attention here by a letter to the *Morning Post* in which he utters a scathing denunciation of the University of Oxford. He claims that at Oxford a student learns nothing. He admits that they go there and they stay there, but he says that during the whole time in Oxford no student ever thinks. In the schools of Texas no student is admitted unless he has passed an examination in thinking and during his entire course thinking is made compulsory at every step. Principal Cactus considers that Oxford dulls a man's mind. He says that after a course at Oxford the student is fit

44

for nothing except the Church or the bar or the House of Lords. He claims that the average Oxford professor would make but a poor showing as a cowboy in Texas."

Education is a splendid topic for this kind of business. But perhaps an even better one is found in getting after our women and girls and denouncing them across the Atlantic. This is always good for ten days excitement. The sample press notice is as follows:—

DENOUNCING AMERICAN GIRLS

New York, April,——

"Lady Violet Longshanks, a direct descendant of Edward I. in the male line, landed yesterday morning in New York from the *Rule Britannia*. Lady Violet has at once excited wide spread comment by an interview which she gave on the dock to a representative of the press. Her ladyship who represents the *haut ton* of the oldest *noblesse* and who is absolutely *carte blanche*, gave expression to a scathing denunciation of the American girl. She declares that the American girl of to-day is without manners. No American girl, the Countess claims, knows how to enter a room, still less how to get out of one. The American girl, according to Lady V. does not know how to use her voice, still less how to use her feet. At the same time the countess expressed herself fascinated with the size of the United States which she considers is undoubtedly a country of the future. Lady V. thinks it probable that many of the shortcomings of the American girl may be due to her habit of chewing tobacco."

And so, of course, as soon as Lady V. has said all this it has to be "mopped up" just like the other stuff. The press sends people to interview five heads of five women's colleges and they all declare that the American girl is as gentle as a lamb, and that if Lady V. really gets to know the American girl she will find that the American girl can use her feet, and will. As to the question of chewing tobacco they need only say that perhaps Lady V. is unaware that in all the first class women's colleges chewing tobacco is expressly forbidden not only on the campus, but in the bedrooms.

This reassures the public and gradually the trouble subsides and everybody cools off and the American girl gets right back to where she was. And then some American lady takes a trip over to England and starts the whole trouble again in a reversed direction, like this:—

DENOUNCES ENGLISH GIRLS

London, April,——

"Mrs. Potter Pancake of Cedar Rapids, Iowa, President of the American Women's International Friendship League, has just jarred English society off its hinges by a sweeping condemnation, handed out from the window of her hotel, directed against English girls. Mrs. Pancake claims that the English girl is absolutely without grace and that her movements are inferior to those of a horse. Mrs. Pancake states further that the English girl moves like an alligator and is unable to sit down. She considers that these defects are mainly caused by drinking gin in inordinate quantities."

Whereupon trouble breaks out all over the

British press from Cornwall to the Orkney Islands. The Archbishop of Canterbury is consulted and issues a statement to the effect that in his opinion the English girl is *more* graceful than a cow and that he has yet to see an English girl of the cultivated class take what *he* considers too much gin. This eases things up a little bit, and the good effect is presently reinforced by a letter to the *Times* from the professor of Orthopedic Surgery at the Royal College of Physicians who says that he has made anthropometric measurements of over a thousand English girls and that their shapes suit *him* down to the ground. After that the trouble blows over and international friendship is just getting settled again and there is every prospect of the payment of the British debt and the scrapping of both navies and the rise of the pound sterling away over par, when someone starts it all off again with this:—

THINKS AMERICANS CROOKED

"Mr. Joseph Squidge, M.P. Labor member for the mining district of Hiddaway-under-the-Sea, has just returned from a three weeks tour of America. Mr. Squidge, who visited the entire United States from New York to Yonkers, has just given an interview to the local paper at Hiddaway in which he says that public honesty is extinct in America. He considers that the entire population of the United States, not excepting the criminal classes, is crooked. He says that in America a man's word is never taken and that even in hotels a guest is required to sign his name."

This of course is too much,—more than any decent people can stand, and as a consequence some one is at once sent over to England, either by accident or by design with the result that in a week or two the whole American press carries a despatch as follows,—

THINKS BRITISH DISHONEST

New York, April,——

"Edward Angle Eye, a journalist representing five thousand American Farmers Newspapers, has just cabled from London to Coffin Creek, Idaho, to say that the British are all liars. He says that with the possible exception of the Prince of

Wales and Queen Mary, it is impossible to trust anybody in the British Isles. Public morality he claims has reached its lowest ebb and is washing away. He attributes the trouble to the large influx of Chinese in London."

———

And after all that, can you wonder if we find it a little hard to keep peace and good will across the Atlantic.

FRENCH POLITICS FOR BEGINNERS

As Explained in a Series of Cables From our Own Special Correspondent in Paris

Paris, 10.30 A. M.

Nothing this morning intimated the imminence of a cabinet crisis. The sky was of spotless serenity, and the whole aspect of the city one of brightness and gayety. The hotels were full of tourists, the shops were crowded, the fountains were running, Punch and Judy was play-

ing in the Champ Elysées, and the French franc
which had shown signs of restlessness the day before had passed a quiet night.

The Chamber of Deputies, however, had
hardly met at 10 o'clock in the Palais Bourbon
when Mr. Painlevé rose in his seat and asked the
premier if he knew what time it was. Mr.
Briand replied that his watch had stopped. Mr.
Painlevé rushing on to the floor in front of the
tribune, demanded from the chamber whether a
man whose watch had stopped was fit to be the
premier of France. Instantly the chamber was
in an uproar. Shouts of "A Bas, Briand,"—were
mingled with cries of "Attaboy, Aristide!"

Mr. Briand, who preserved throughout the
most complete calm, then asked for a vote of
the chamber. The vote at once showed that not
only was the whole of the Left side against Mr.
Briand but also a bit of the Center and the East
and South and some of the North-West. Mr.
Briand immediately resigned and the great government which had presided over the destiny
of France and weathered every storm for six days,
went out of office.

51

Paris, 12.30 P. M.

It has now been learned that on the news of Mr. Briand's resignation the President of the Republic summoned Mr. Painlevé to the Palace of the Elysées and asked him if he could form a cabinet. On Mr. Painlevé asking for time the President said that he could have twenty minutes. Mr. Painlevé drove at once to the Chamber of Deputies and, crossing the floor of the house where Mr. Briand sat, kissed him on both cheeks and asked him if he would join his government. Mr. Briand, having thrown his arms around Mr. Painlevé, announced his willingness to join him. Within a few moments the chamber was informed of the formation of the Painlevé-Briand ministry, the news being greeted with acclamation.

THE PAINLEVÉ-BRIAND MINISTRY

The president of the session having announced a ten minutes adjournment to allow the new ministry to make a budget, it became clear that the Painlevé-Briand ministry would find itself in a position of great strength. It will have the support of the whole radical bloc, together with a

chunk of Socialists and about half a bloc of con-
servatives.   No French government, for the last
six months, has been in such a position of power.
Briand, it is said with great satisfaction, will be
virtually a dictator over the destinies of France.
As soon as the news was disseminated on the
Bourse the franc humped itself up two and a half
points.

Paris, 11.45 A. M.

Mr. Briand and Mr. Painlevé, entering the
chamber with their arms round one another's
waists, read out their budget to a breathless
house.   The aim of the new government will be
to put the finances of France on a basis of absolute stability.   To do this they will at once borrow 4,000,000,000 francs.   The loan, however,
will be offset and made good by a credit with the
Bank of France, which will then float a loan with
the public, who will then be authorised, by a de-
cree, to borrow from the bank.   The entire credit
thus created will be added up and declared ex-
tinguished.   The announcement of the budget
policy was received with a salvo of enthusiasm,
the entire left embracing the whole of the right.

53

FALL OF THE GOVERNMENT

Paris, 12.30 P. M.

The Briand-Painlevé government has fallen.
Entrenched in power as it seemed behind a solid
parliamentary support, it fell suddenly and un-
expectedly on an interpellation during the budget
debate. Mr. Raymond Poincaré, who is generally regarded as the master mind of French
politics, rose during the discussion of budget and
asked whether the government intended to retain
the tax on beer. On Mr. Briand's saying that it
was proposed to keep this tax, Mr. Poincaré declared that the true national policy would be to
let the Germans drink enough beer to pay taxes
for both nations. If they couldn't do it they
should be made to. The whole chamber seethed
with enthusiasm, during which Mr. Briand and
Mr. Painlevé announced that their government
was at an end. The president of the chamber,
calling for order amid the tumult, asked if there
was any gentleman present who could form a new
government. Mr. Poincaré offered to do so if
the president would let him talk with Mr. Pain-

levé and Mr. Briand outside for a few minutes.
The permission being given the three statesmen
shortly afterward reentered the chamber and announced that they had succeeded in combining
themselves into a ministry to be called the Poin-
caré-Painlevé-Briand Ministry.

POINCARÉ-PAINLEVÉ-BRIAND MINISTRY

Mr. Poincaré said, however, that they would
only do this if they could be assured of a block
behind them.   If there was no block they wouldn't
be a ministry.   The enthusiasm of the Left together with part of the Right and a little bit of
the Top, made it clear that the new ministry will
receive an ample support.   An adjournment was
made with universal congratulations.

FALL OF THE FRENCH MINISTRY

Paris, 3.30 P. M.

The new French government, which was
formed by Mr. Poincaré with the support of Mr.
Painlevé and Mr. Briand fell right after lunch.
Details are yet lacking.   Apparently it came into

the chamber after lunch and fell.   There is a general consternation.   The Bourse is wildly excited and all the exchanges reacted sharply.   It is said that the Governor of the Bank of France will be arrested and perhaps the Archbishop of Paris. It is whispered that the fall of the ministry was occasioned by Mr. Joseph Caillaux, who seated himself in the chamber and looked at the ministry with that inscrutable look which he has, till it fell.

THE CAILLAUX-POINCARÉ-PAINLEVÉ-BRIAND MINISTRY

Paris, 4.15 P. M.

A certain measure of calm has been restored in Paris by the announcement that an entirely new ministry has been formed by the union of Mr. Caillaux—Mr. Poincaré—Mr. Painlevé and Mr. Briand.   In a statement to the press Mr. Briand said that the old government had outlived its usefulness and that he welcomed the addition of Mr. Caillaux.   A new budget would be made at once and would constitute, he said, the best budget of the last three weeks. This budget, which will absolutely ensure the stability of French finance will be based on a vote of National Credit supported by a Universal Loan and guaranteed by a Public Debt. Mr. Caillaux, whose financial genius never shone more brightly, is working out a tax, to replace the proposed capital levy and the income tax, and to be called the Tax on Somebody Else.

It is said in well informed circles that if the government can be widened to include a royalist element and to take in a few communists and a bloc of socialists, its success will be assured. If it can then pursue a policy which will be sufficiently clerical and conservative while at the same time strongly socialist, with a touch of opportunism, it may last till Saturday.

Meantime the theatres are all open, work is plentiful, everybody is happy, Paris is bright with spring flowers, the hotels are full of Americans dripping with money, the new fashions are said to be simply charming, the skirts don't reach anywhere, the watering places are wetter than ever, —so what does a little thing like a government matter?

57

THE MOTHER OF PARLIAMENTS

*But what has lately gone Wrong with
Mother?*

"The House of Commons," says the well
known *Guide Book to London of Today,* "not
inaptly called the Mother of Parliaments, is undoubtedly the most august, as it is the most vener-
able, of the great representative assemblies of
the world. It is with something like awe that we
penetrate into the stillness of Westminster Palace,
and find ourselves presently looking down from
our privileged place in the gallery upon the earnest group of men whose measured tones and
dignified formalities are deciding the fate of an
empire."

That is what the Guide Book has been saying
about the House of Commons for some two hundred years. But in reading over the press reports of the debates of the House within the last
year or so as they come across the Atlantic, one
is inclined to wonder whether the cold dignity of
the dear old place is not getting a little thawed
out in the warm times in which we live.

The proceedings in the later days sound a little too suggestive of the Cowboys Convention of Montana, or the meeting of the Literary and Philosophical Society of Dawson City, Yukon.

Take in illustration the following report of the proceedings of one day some months ago, taken verbatim from the *London Times* and the *London Morning Post* or the *Labor Herald*—I forget which. At any rate, those who read the debates of the house will recognize it at once as genuine.

"The House of Commons resumed its session yesterday at three o'clock. The Prime Minister in rising from the Treasury Benches to present his bill for the introduction of Buckwheat into the Tanganyika district of Uganda, stated that he would like first to refer to the fact that some member of the House had just thrown a banana at the Speaker. He would ask members to realize that throwing bananas at the Speaker impeded the business of the House. He would go so far as to say that it was bad manners.

"At the word 'manners' the House broke into an uproar. Cries arose from the labor benches, 'Manners! Yah! Manners!'

"Lady Luster at once leapt to her feet and said

59

that there were members in the House whose manners were not fit for a stable.

"Joseph Dockside, M.P. for the Buckingham Palace district, asked if she meant him. Lady Luster called out that she did. The Speaker rose to a ruling against personal mention quoting a precedent under Henry VIII. But another banana hit him and he sat down.

"Mr. Dockside began to cry. He asked the House if it was fair to let an idle woman like Lady Luster tell him that he had no manners. He was only a poor man and had no schooling, and how could he even get a chance to pick up manners, even fit for a stable. Here he broke into sobs again while the labor benches resounded with the cries of 'Shame!' and the blowing of horns.

"Lady Luster then said that she had gone too far. She would take back the word stable. She meant 'Garage.'

"The Speaker, quoting a precedent from Edward the Confessor, said that the debate might go on—a pineapple hitting him in the waistcoat just before, and as, he sat down.

"The Prime Minister then said that as quiet had been restored (loud cries of *Rah! Rah!*

Quiet!,) he would resume his speech on the pro-
posal of the government to subsidize the growing buckwheat—and he would add, buckoats—in
the Tanganyika district.

"At this point he was interrupted by Colonel
MacAlpin MacFoozle, independent member for
the East Riding of the West Hebrides. The
Colonel wanted to know how the Prime Minister
could speak of Tanganyika if he was fully aware
of the condition of Scotland. Did he know of
the present distress among the crofters? Was
he aware of what was happening to the Scottish
gillies, and the Laddies and Collies?

"Did he know that three more men had left
the Hebrides? The Colonel, who spoke with
violent passion, to the great delight of the House,
said that he didn't give a curse for buckwheat or
for Tanganyika and that personally he could lick
the whole cabinet.

"At this, loud shouts of *'Attaboy! You're the
Hot Stuff,'* were mingled with cries of *'Put him
out!'* Lady Luster called out that if the Scots
would quit drinking Scotch whiskey they would
all save enough money to leave Scotland.

"For the moment, the transaction of public

business was seriously threatened when Lord Pintop Daffodil rose and asked the Speaker's leave
to tell a funny story. Lord Pintop, who is rapidly gaining the reputation of being the third
funniest member of the House, was greeted with
encouraging laughter and applause.

"The Speaker having ruled that a funny story
had been told under Queen Anne, Lord Pintop
then related a story of how a Pullman car pas-
senger was put off at Buffalo by the porter. The
House, which is easily moved from anger to mer-
riment and which enjoys nothing (except its
lunch) so much as a good joke, was convulsed
with laughter.

"The Speaker, in thanking the honorable member for the story, said that he believed that it was
the same story as was told under Queen Anne.

"The Prime Minister then said he would resume his speech on buckwheat. He was about
to do so when Mr. Ilyitch Halfoff, member for
the Russian district of Westminster, said that he
would like first to rise and present a resolution
for the immediate introduction of communism
into England. The House was in a turmoil in a
minute.

"Cries of *'Russia for Ever!!'* were mixed with the singing of the *'Marseillaise'* and the counter-singing of *'Scots Whoo Hoo!'* It was said afterwards that the singing was the best ever heard in the House this month.

"At this point in the debate the yeoman usher of the Black Stick rushed into the House and called— 'Hurry out, Boys, there is a circus procession coming down Whitehall!' The whole House rushed out in a body, only the speaker remaining behind for one minute to adjourn the session."

NEW LIGHT FROM NEW MINDS

A Study in International Interviews

People who read the newspapers regularly must have noticed that the reported Interviews are getting to be much brighter and more interesting than they used to be. Till recently, when the press interviewed travellers, distinguished visitors and political emissaries, they talked to each of them about his own particular line of life and the things about which he was supposed to know something. The result was fearful dulness. A director of the Bank of England was interviewed about currency, an actor was interviewed about the stage and a bishop about religion. As a consequence every one of them got prosy and unintelligible.

Nowadays the thing is done in exactly the other way. Each distinguished visitor is asked questions about something that is outside of his own line of life. A vaudeville comedian gives his impressions of French Politics and an English Bishop gives his views of women's skirts. The result is a freshness and a charm which lends a new attraction to our newspapers on both sides of the Atlantic. Here are a few examples taken from the current press and drawn, as appears at once, indifferently from England and America.

Ball Player Visits St. Paul's

London, Friday. Ed. Lanigan, star outfielder and manager of the Tuscaloosa Base Ball Nine, passed through London this morning and expressed himself as delighted with it. After he had had a run round town, Ed. gave his views, on

some of the things he had seen, to a crowd of
assembled admirers at the Hotel Cecil. "What
did you think of St. Paul's, Ed?" asked one of
the boys. "It's certainly big stuff," said Ed.
"and it gets me. Those old geysers certainly
knew how to build. And I want to tell you boys
that there's something about that building that
you don't get everyday. I doubt if there are a
dozen men in New York to-day who could du-
plicate it."

"How does the political situation in England
strike you," he was next queried. "Fine!" answered the big man. "They've sure got a lot of
taxes here. But then mind you there's a lot of
wealth too. Of course things are pretty bad, but
you've got to remember they were bad before,
and anyway they're not so bad."

Movie Star Sees Riviera

Mentone, Monday. Gus Phinn, the well
known movie star who is said to command a salary
of anywhere from half a million dollars, was a recent visitor at Mentone. Gus is enthusiastic over
the Mediterranean sea. "I want to tell you right

now," he said to a representative of the press, "that there is absolutely nothing wrong with the Mediterranean." "What did you specially notice about it, Gus?" asked the pressman. "Why, what gets me hardest is the colour of the water. Say, I don't think you can beat that blue anywhere. You might try but you can't do it." "Do you think," asked another of the group, "that the tone of English Social Life is deteriorating?" "No, I don't," Gus replied. "I think the tone is good. I think it A.1."

"What about the relations of England and France, Gus?" was another question. "They're all right," the star answered. "We met a lot of French boys on the boat and certainly nicer boys you wouldn't want to meet. Well, they're gentlemen that's what they are. The French are gentlemen.

"What about Germans, Gus?" one of the reporters ventured.

"All right!" answered the movie man heartily. "We had a German at our table in the hotel and they're all right. Mind you I think we were perfectly right in crushing them because they needed to be crushed. But they're all right."

Copper King Looks at Oxford

Oxford, Tuesday. E. J. Slagg, the multimillionaire owner of mines and president of Slagg Consolidated Copper, visited Oxford yesterday and was shown round the colleges. The big copper man whose quiet taciturnity and power of silence has made him the terror of the stock exchange, looked about him at everything with the same keen shrewdness with which he detects a vein of copper under a hundred feet of trap rock. Only now and then he darted a shrewd question or let fall a short comment.

"This place," he said, "is old." On the threshold of the Bodleian Library he paused a moment as if rapidly measuring the contents with his eye. "Mostly books?" he asked. The copper king also paused a moment before the monument erected to the memory of Latimer and Ridley. "What's the idea?" he asked.

. . . .

But,—as I said up above this new and brilliant flood of light is not only turned on Europe. By a similar process it is let loose on the American continent too.

67

British Lord Sees Jersey Tugs

New York, Wednesday. Lord Tinklepin who arrived from England on the *Aquitania* yesterday was taken for a trip up and down the harbour in a fast tug. His lordship expressed himself as amazed at the commerce of New York. "I had no idea of it," he said. Passing by one of the car ferries of the Erie Railway, Lord Tinklepin expressed the keenest interest. "What the devil is that?" he asked. On being told what it was, the distinguished visitor who is well known for his interest in physical science, at once asked "why doesn't it upset?"

Lady Visitor Discusses American Banking

New York, Thursday. Lady Mary Messabout, President of the Women's Federation for Universal Mutual Understanding, was shown round financial New York yesterday as the guest of the Bankers Association. Lady Mary expressed the greatest wonder at the Sub-Treasury of the United States. "Is it possible" she said, "that it's full of money?" Lady Mary was questioned by representatives of the press as to her opinion of the American banking system. "It is really excellent," she answered, "so little delay and such civility everywhere." "Do you think," —it was asked by a member of the press,— "that the deflation of American currency would check the expansion of business." "Oh, I hope not," Lady Mary answered warmly, "surely it would never do that."

French Baron Visits West

Saskatoon, Saskatchewan, Friday. The Baron de Vieux Chateau, who is visiting Saskatchewan with a view to seeing whether the richer parts of Canada would be suited for the poorer class of Frenchmen, was taken yesterday on a tour of inspection of the grain elevators of Saskatoon. "But they are marvellous!" the Baron said to a member of the press on his return to his hotel. "They seem to me absolutely,—how shall I say it,—enormous." In further discussion the Baron said the whole system of distributing the wheat seemed to him excellent. When asked what his impression of the Farmer's Cooperative movement was, the distinguished visitor again spoke with enthusiasm. "But your farmers!" he said, "they are wonderful! what courage! what tenacity! to have come here and stayed here! It is wonderful."

AN ADVANCE CABLE SERVICE

International News a Month Ahead

It has recently become the habit to send out and circulate all sorts of special information in the form of "services." The schools of commerce send out "financial services" with a forecast of business conditions six months before they happen and some times even six months before they don't happen. The departments of agriculture send out crop reports even before the grain is planted. The meteorologists keep at least a fortnight ahead of the weather. Political forecasts are now ready for all the elections up to 1928. The hard winter that is going to begin about Xmas time has been definitely prophesied, in fact promised by the squirrels, the groundhogs and the makers of fur garments and by the West Indian Steamship agents.

It has occurred to me that a useful extension might be made to these "services" by adding an *Advance European Cable Service*. By this means all readers of newspapers, instead of having to read the cables day by day, could get them in a lump a month at a time. Anybody who has studied the newspapers of the last three or four years recognises at once that the cables run in a regular round, quite easy to prophesy. In the modest little attempt appended below, I have endeavoured to put in merely the ordinary routine of European public life for one month without prophesying anything of an exceptional or extreme character.

German Revolution Coming

Berlin, Monday 1. A monarchical wave is reported as having swept over Germany. The wildest excitement prevails. A hundred persons were trampled to death in Berlin the other day. The return of His Imperial Majesty the Kaiser is expected at any moment.

71

And Going

Berlin, Tuesday 2. A republican wave has swept over Germany in the place of the monarchical wave of yesterday. Another hundred people were trampled to death. William Hohenzollern is reported as still at Doorn in Holland.

And Has Gone

Berlin, Wednesday 3. Germany is quiet. Christmas shopping is beginning already. Everywhere there is cheerfulness and optimism. Nobody was trampled to death all day.

Frenzied Finance in France

Paris, Thursday 4. Following on the sensational statement of Monsieur Caillaux that France would pay her debts to the last penny, the wildest excitement prevailed on the Bourse. The franc which had been fairly steady all yesterday, rose to its feet, and staggered right across the street where it collapsed in a heap. Gloom prevails in financial circles.

Paris, Friday 5. Monsieur Caillaux has issued a supplementary statement to the effect that France will pay all her debts but it may take her a million years to do it. This assurance has restored universal confidence and Monsieur Caillaux is hailed everywhere as having redeemed the honor and credit of France. A tremendous ovation was given him today when eating a sandwich at the lunch counter. It is now said that Caillaux, who is recognised everywhere as the financial saviour of France, is working out a plan for wiping out the whole debt of France by borrowing it from England.

Home Life in England

London, Saturday 6. England is face to face with a coal strike of such magnitude that in twenty-four hours every fire in England will go out. If the transport workers and the public house keepers join the strike the whole industrial life of the nation will come to a full stop. Meantime the Archbishop of Canterbury says that if he can't get a satchelful of nut coal tonight he must close the cathedral.

73

London, Monday 8. The coal strike was called off at five minutes before midnight,—one of the closest shaves of a total collapse of England that has been reported in the last six months. Meantime with cloudless skies and bright sunshine the whole attention of the nation today is riveted on the champion football game between the Huddersfield and Hopton-under-Lime. The Archbishop of Canterbury will kick off the ball.

Italian Upheaval Heaving Up

Rome, Tuesday 9. The Italian Fascisti have broken loose again. Yesterday a man climbed up to the top of the Duomo at Milan and waved a black shirt, shouting EVIVA ITALIA! The whole nation is in a ferment. Anything may happen.

Rome, Wednesday 10. It is all right. It transpires that the shirt was not black, it was merely very dirty.

Austria in Chaos

Vienna, Thursday 11. Mr. Edward Edelstein, vice-president of the Canned Soup Company

of Paterson, New Jersey who is making a ten day
tour in central Europe to study business conditions, describes the situation of Austria as one
of utter chaos. Trade is absolutely stagnant.
Business is almost extinct while the currency is
in entire confusion. In Vienna unemployment is
everywhere, even the rich are eating in soup
kitchens; the theatres are closed and social life
is paralyzed.

Complete Revival of Austria

Vienna, Friday 12. Mr. John Smithers of
Smitherstown, who is taking a five days vacation in Europe reports that the economic situation of Austria has been reestablished on a sound
basis. The restoration of the currency this morning by the establishment of a new and easier
mark, is working wonders. The factories are
running on full time, the shops are crowded with
visitors, the hotels are bursting with guests and
the theatres are offering *Shakespeare, Grand
Opera,* and *Uncle Tom's Cabin.*

Vienna, Saturday 5. Austria has collapsed
again.

Dear Old Russia

Petrograd (otherwise Leningrad or Trotskiville), Monday 15. Reports from the Caucasus say that Red forces made a drive at the Caucasians yesterday. The latter just got out of the road in time.

Tuesday 16. Word has been received that the Reds made a fierce drive at Semipalatinsk. They only got half of it.

Wednesday 17. Wireless despatches say that the Reds are preparing for a drive against the Persians. Most of the Persians have already climbed up Mount Ararat.

Thursday 18. It is reported that the Council of Workmens Soviets of Moskow have passed a resolution declaring that universal peace has come.

International Goodwill

Tokio, Friday 19. Viscount Itch, is reported in the Japanese *Daily Hootch* as saying that the time has come when Japan can not tolerate the existence of the United States on the other side of the Pacific. It will have to be moved. Wild excitement prevailed after the delivery of the speech. Enormous crowds paraded the streets of Tokio, shouting "Down with America!" An American missionary was chased into a Chinese restaurant.

Tokio, Saturday 20. Viscount Itch has issued a statement to the effect that Japan and the United States are sisters. Wild enthusiasm prevails. Great crowds are parading the streets, shouting "Attaboi Coolidji!" The missionary has come down again.

Yokohama, Monday 22. The business section of Yokohama was destroyed yesterday by an earthquake.

Yokohama, Tuesday 23. The business section of Yokohama has been propped up again and nailed into position.

From the Far Away South Seas

London, Wednesday 24. Cable advices received via Fiji and Melbourne report the Marquesas Islanders in a plebiscite have voted for prohibition, direct legislation, proportional representation and the abolition of cannibalism. Some more votes will be taken next week.

BACK FROM EUROPE

The Reaction of Travel on the Human Mind

There comes a time every year when all the hundreds of thousands of people who have been over to Europe on a summer tour get back again. It is very generally supposed that a tour of this kind ought to have a broadening effect on the mind, and this idea is vigorously propagated by the hotel companies at Schlitz, Bitz, Biarritz, and picturesque places of that sort.

It is not for me to combat this idea. But I do know that in certain cases at least a trip to Europe sets up a distinct disturbance of the intellect. Some of these afflictions are so well defined that they could almost be definitely classified as diseases. I will quote only a few among the many examples that might be given.

78

Back from Europe

I

ARISTOCROPSIS, OR WEAKENING OF THE BRAIN
FROM CONTACT WITH THE BRITISH
ARISTOCRACY.

There seems to be no doubt that a sudden
contact with the titled classes disturbs the nerve
cells or ganglions of the traveler from America,
and brings on a temporary enfeeblement of mind.
It is generally harmless, especially as it is usually
accompanied by an extreme optimism and an exaggerated sense of importance.

*Specimen Case. Winter conversation of Mr.
John W. Axman, retired hardware millionaire of
Fargo, Dakota, in regard to his visit to England.*

．　　．　　．　　．　　．　　．　　．

"I don't know whether I told you that I saw
a good deal of the Duke of Dumpshire while I
was in England. In fact, I went to see him at
his seat—all these dukes have seats, you know.
You can say what you like about the British
aristocrats, but when you meet one like the Duke
of Dumpshire, they are all right. Why, he was

just as simple as you or me, or simpler. When he met me, he said, 'How are you?' Just like that.

"And then he said, 'You must be hungry. Come along and let's see if we can find some cold beef.' Just as easy as that. And then he said to a butler or someone, 'Go and see if you can find some cold beef.' And presently the butler came back and said, 'There's some cold beef on the table, Sir,' and the Duke said, 'All right, let's go and eat it.' And he went and sat right down in front of the beef and ate it. Just as you or I would.

"All the time we were eating it, the Duke was talking and laughing. He's got a great sense of humor, the Duke has. After he'd finished the beef, he said, 'Well, that was a darn good piece of beef!' and of course we both roared. The Duke's keen on politics, too—right up to date about everything. 'Let's see,' he said, 'who's your President now?' In fact, he's just as keen as mustard, and looks far ahead too. 'France,' he said to me, 'is in for a hell of a time.' "

II

NUTTOLINGUALISM, OR LOSS OF ONE'S OWN LANGUAGE AFTER THREE WEEKS ACROSS THE SEA

Specimen No. I. Verbatim statement of Mr. Phin Gulch, college student from Umskegee College, Oklahoma, made immediately on his return from a three weeks athletic tour in England with Oklahoma Olympic Aggregation. "England certainly is a ripping place. The chaps we met were simply topping. Of course here and there one met a bounder, but on the whole one was treated absolutely top hole."

Specimen No. 2. Information in regard to French restaurants supplied by Miss Phoebe McGinn, winner of the Beauty Contest Ticket to Europe and Back from Boom City, Montana. "The Paris restaurants are just charming and ever so cheap if you know where to go. There was one we used to go to in a little rue close to the gare where we got our dejeuner with croissants and cafe au lait for soixante quinze centimes.

81

"Of course we used to give the garcon another quinze centimes as a pourboire. And after dejeuner we'd sit there half the matinee and read the journaux and watch the people go past in the rue. Always, when we left, the garcon would say, 'Au revoir.' Regular French, you know."

III

MEGALOGASTRIA, OR DESIRE TO TALK ABOUT FOOD

Specimen Case. Mr. Hefty Undercut, of Saskatoon, Saskatchewan, retired hotel man, talks on European culture.

"I don't mind admitting that the English seem to me away ahead of us. They're further on. They know how to do things better. Now you take beefsteak. They cut it half as thick again as we do, and put it right on a grid over hot coals. They keep the juice in it. Or take a mutton chop. The way they cook them over there, you can eat two pounds to one that you eat here. You see they're an older people than we are.

"Or take sausages—when I travel I like to observe everything; it makes you broader—and I've noticed their sausages are softer than ours, more flavoring to them. Or take one of those big deep meat pies—why, they eat those big pies at midnight. You can do it there. The climate's right for it.

"And, as I say, when I travel I go around noticing everything and sizing everything up—the meat, the lobsters, the kind of soup they have, everything. You see, over there there's very little sunlight and the air is heavy and you eat six times a day. It's a great place."

INTROSPEXOSIS, OR SEEING IN OTHER PEOPLE WHAT IS REALLY IN YOURSELF

It appears that many people when they travel really see nothing at all except the reflection of their own ideas. They think that what they are interested in is uppermost everywhere. They might just as well stay at home and use a looking glass. Take in witness,

The evidence of Mr. Soggie Spinnage, Secretary of the Vegetarian Society of North, Cen-

*tral, and South America, as given after his return
from a propaganda tour in England.*

.   .   .   .

"Oh, there's no doubt the vegetarian movement is spreading in England. We saw it everywhere. At Plymouth a man came right up to
me and he said, 'Oh, my dear Brother, I wish
we had a thousand men here like you. Go back,'
he said, 'go back and bring over a thousand
others.' And wherever I spoke I met with such
enthusiasm.

"I spoke, I remember, in Tooting-on-the-
Hump—it's within half an hour of London itself. And when I looked into their dear faces
and told them about the celery in Kalamazoo,
Michigan, and about the big cabbages in the
South Chicago mud flats, they just came flocking
about me! 'Go back,' they said, 'go back and
send those over.'

"I heard a man in a restaurant one day say to
the waiter, 'Just fetch me a boiled cabbage. I
want nothing else.' I went right up to him, and
I took his hand and I said, 'Oh, my dear friend,
I have come all the way from America just to

84

hear that.' And he said, 'Go back,' he said, 'go back and tell them that you've heard it.'

"Why, when you go to England you just see vegetables, vegetables, everywhere. I hardly seemed to see anything else. They say even the King eats vegetables now. And they say the Bishop of London only eats beans. I heard someone say that the Bishop seemed full of beans all the time.

"Really I felt that the cause was just gaining and growing all the time. When I came to leave, a little group of friends come down to the steamer to say good-bye. 'Go back,' they said, 'go back and send someone else.'

"That seemed to be the feeling everywhere."

III
STUDIES IN THE NEWER CULTURE

A Little Study in Culture from Below Up

ABOUT fifteen years ago somebody invented the word *Attaboy*. At first it was used only by the urchins on the baseball bleachers. Presently it was used by the college students. After that it was taken up by business men, lawyers, judges and congressmen and it spread all over the world.

It is said that when King George of England welcomed home General Allenby after his conquest of Palestine, he put his hands on Allenby's shoulders and said with deep feeling, "Attaboy!"

The General, profoundly touched, was heard to murmur in return, "Some King, what!"

This story may or may not be true. It is possible that King George used merely some such dignified English phrase as "Not half bad at all!" But the story at any rate illustrates the tremendous change that has been creeping over our language.

I am not here referring to the use of slang. That of course is as old as language itself. The man who uses a slang word and, let us say, calls a man's hat his *"lid"* or calls a woman a *"skirt,"* is unconscious of using a metaphor and of trying to be funny or peculiar. But the man who uses *attaboy* language in speech or writing is really trying to say something; he really thinks he is using English. It is not merely the words that he uses but the way in which he uses them.

Let me give an instance,—that is much quicker business than trying to explain the whole thing in a methodical fashion.

Attaboy Letter of Invitation

Here for example,—to illustrate the old style of writing and speaking,—is a letter which I received almost thirty years ago inviting me to attend a gathering of my college class. In point of dignity and good form the letter speaks for itself.

TORONTO, Feb. 1st, 1896.

DEAR SIR:

I beg to inform you that a reunion of the

90

graduating class of 1891 will be held on the 5th of February in the form of a dinner at the Queen's Hotel. The guest of honor on the occasion will be Professor Baxter, who has kindly consented to deliver an address to the class. It is confidently expected that all the members of the class will take this opportunity to renew old friendships. The price of the dinner, including wines, will be seventy-five cents. May I ask you to send a reply at your earliest convenience.

With sincere personal regards,
I have the honor to be
And to remain being
Yours very faithfully,
JOHN SMITH.

Now it happened that just the other day I received a letter from the same old classmate inviting me to attend a similar gathering of the class, —thirty years later. But here is how he has expressed the invitation——

Mr. He-Man from College!
This is You!
Say! what do you think? The real old He-Boys of 1891 are going to gather in for a feed at the

Queen's on February 5th. Songs! Speeches!
Fireworks! And who do you think is going to
be the main Big Talk! You'd never guess,—
why old Prof Baxter—old nutsey Baxter!
Come and hear him. Come along right now!
The whole feed,—songs, fun and smokes included
—is only six bucks. So get down in your pants
and fork them out.

Yours, Attaboy! Hooroo!
Rev. John Smith,
(Canon of the Cathedral)

An Attaboy Dictionary

Let it be noted that the great point of the *Attaboy* system is the terrific desire for emphasis.
A man is not called a man. He is called a *He-
man*. Even that is not enough. He has to be
100 *per cent* he-man. And in extreme cases he
must be called a "100 per cent, full blooded, bull-
chested, big-headed, great-hearted man,"—all of
this to replace the simple old-fashioned word
gentleman.

Indeed, one could write quite a little dictionary
of Attaboy terms like this,——

GENTLEMAN—(See above.)

LADY—a big-hearted, wide-eyed, warm-chested woman, a hundred per cent soul, and built square.

FRIEND—a he-man with a hand-grip and a jaw that means that as soon as you see him in front of you, you know that he is back of you.

SENATOR—far-sighted, frog-eyed, nation-making he-man.

CRIMINAL—no such word. Try "hold-up man"—"yegg"—"thug"—"expert safe-cracker," etc., etc., etc.

In the same way when the *Attaboy* language turns from the nouns to the verbs there has to be the same vital emphasis. The fatal step was taken when someone invented the word *punch*. Since then every form of action has to be described as if it occurred with a direct physical shock. A speaker has got to *hit* his audience with a *punch*, he must *lift* them, throw them, in short fairly *kick* them out of the room.

A book is said to be *arresting, gripping, compelling*. It has got to hold the reader down so that he can't get up. A preacher has got to be *vital, dynamic;* he must *put his sermon over;* he must pitch it at the audience; in short, preaching becomes a form of baseball with the clergyman in the box.

In other words the whole of our life and thought has got to be restated in terms of moving things, in terms of electricity, radio and all the crackling physical apparatus of the world in which we live.

Macaulay and Gibbon in Attaboy

It is quite clear that if this *Attaboy* tendency goes on all the books of the past will have to be rewritten or nobody will understand them. Somebody will have to re-edit them so as to put into them the necessary "pep" and "punch" to make them readable by the next generation.

We can imagine how completely unintelligible will be the stately pages of such dignified writers as Macaulay or Gibbon. Here, for example, is a specimen of the way in which Gibbon's "Decline and Fall of The Roman Empire" will be revised. I take as an illustration a well known passage describing the action of a heroic matron of Rome

94

in rallying the wavering citizens after a retreat. It runs:

"A Roman matron of imposing appearance and striking countenance stepped forth before the hesitating citizens,——"

Translation:

"A pre-war blonde who was evidently a real peach skipped out in front of the bunch,——"

"At the sight of her the citizens paused——"

Translation:

"As soon as they put their lamps on her all the guys stood still,——"

"Reluctant cries of admiration arose from the crowd——"

" 'Some doll!' said the boys."

" 'Cowards!' she exclaimed."

" 'You big stiffs,' she snorted."

" 'And would you leave the defense of your homes at such a time as this!' "

" 'Do you mean to say that you are going to fly the coop?' "

" 'To your posts all of you!' she cried."

" 'Beat it,' she honked."

"Inspired by her courage the citizens with

95

shouts of 'Long Live Sempronia!' rushed to the ramparts."

"Full of pep they all shouted, 'Attaboy, Lizzie!' and skipped up the ladders."

Rome was Saved

Epitaph on an Attaboy

Even the epitaphs on the grave stones will have to be altered. The old style used to run, "Here lies the body of John Smith, who was born on February 1, 1802 and departed this life on December 1, 1861. He was a loving son, a fond parent, a devoted husband and a patriotic citizen. This stone has been erected by his mourning widow to commemorate his many virtues and in the expectation of his resurrection."

But that kind of thing will have to be replaced by an epitaph with more "punch" in it, something more "gripping," more compelling. Try this:

"*Mr. Passerby! Stop! This is for you,—* you *careless HOG.*

"*Read it.*

"*Here lies a cookoo, John Smith, one of the real boys. He opened his lamps first on Febru-*

ary 1, 1802.   He stepped off the big plank into the dark stuff on December 1, 1861—   But when the big Horn calls 'ALL UP,' oh, say, ATTA-BOY!"

THE CROSSWORD PUZZLE CRAZE

"I beg your pardon," said a man sitting opposite to me in the smoking end of a Pullman car. "Do you happen to know the name of an Arabian Feudal Ruler in five letters?"

"Yes," I said, "a sheik."

He wrote the word down in a notebook that was spread out upon his knee. Then he said,

"And what's the Hottentot house on the move in five letters?"

"A Kraal," I answered.

"Oh—yes, Kraal!" he said. "I could only think of a bungalow; and here's another that's a regular bowler, what is an extinct graminiferous lizard in thirteen letters?"

"Ichthyosaurus," I said.

"How's that?" he asked.   "My, I wish I'd had a college education,—let me write it down— wait now—I-c-h-t-, —say, I believe it's going to

97

get it—yes, sir, it's getting it— By Gee! It's got it. It all fits in now except there's a dirty little hitch in this corner. Say, could there be any word in three letters that would be e-k-e?"

"Yes," I said, " 'eke,' it means 'also.' "

"Then I've got the whole thing—just in time— here's my station. Say, I'm ever so much obliged. I guess I will have one on the wife when I show her this. That's a peach, that ichthy-what d'ye call it. Good-bye."

He left me and I knew that I had been dealing with another of the new victims of the cross-word puzzle mania. I knew that as soon as he got into his house he would work the ichthyo-saurus on his wife; indeed he would probably find her seated with a paper and pencil trying to figure out whether the Icelandish skol will fit in with a form of religion called "Tosh." The thing generally runs in families.

This crossword puzzle is said to have originated in Thibet. From there it was transferred to the Mongolians who introduced it to the Hairy Ainus of Japan, who were delighted with it, as they naturally would be. From them it crossed the ocean to the Siwash Indians who passed it on to the Dog Ribs and to the Flat Heads, and in this way it got to the American Colleges.

The mania has now assumed international dimensions. It is estimated that if the cross-word puzzle solvers were stood up in line (either horizontally or vertically, they wouldn't care which), they would reach half way to Havana. Some might even get there.

But the greatest thing about the crossword puzzle is the way in which it is brightening up our language. Old words that had been forgotten for five hundred years are being polished up as bright as new. A man no longer says, "Good morning. How are you?" he says, "Good morn. How fare you?" And the other man answers that he feels yardly and eke his wife, especially as they expect eft soon to take a holy day and make a cast to Atlantic City.

Before this thing began there were lots of people so ignorant that they didn't know what "Yost" meant, or what a "farrago" is, or which part of a dog is its "withers." Now these are family words. Anyone would say quite naturally, "Just give that dog a kick in the farrago and put him out."

I notice especially the general improvement in exact knowledge for the names of animals and parts of animals. Who used to know what a *marsupial* was? Who could have told where the *dewlap* of an ox is? How many people had heard of the *carapace* of the mud turtle, or knew how to give a proper name to the east ear of an elephant?

Many crossword puzzle experts go further. When engaged in conversation they don't even need to use the very words they mean. They merely indicate them in crossword puzzle fashion and the expert listening to them can solve their conversation at once. Here is a sample of the new,——

Crossword Puzzle Conversation

"Good morning, Short-for-Peter."

"Hullo, Diminutive-of-William. How do you experience-a-sensation in four letters this morning?"

"Worse than a word in four letters rhyming with *bell* and *tell*."

"Oh, I am sorry to hear it. What is the substance, body or cubic content of space in six letters with you?"

"Cold in the bronchial tunnels, passages, or English name for a subway."

"Possessing or exhibiting grace with the personal adjective! Who is treating you?"

"Only the woman in four letters bound to me by law for life!"

"Indeed! Surely you ought not to be an adverb in three letters in this weather."

"No, I ought to be a preposition in two. But I have to go to my effort, energy or mental or bodily exertion undertaken for gain in four letters."

"Well, take good care of yourself. Good remain with you as a form of exclamation used in parting in seven letters."

There are evidently large possibilities in this form of speech. I think that a lot of our literature could be brightened up with words of romance and mystery by putting it into crossword puzzle language.

Crossword Poetry

Even our poetry would be none the worse for it. Here, for example, is a once familiar bit of Longfellow's verse turned into this kind of dialect:

Under the spreading chestnut tree,
The village smithy remains erect, upright or in a vertical
    position common to man and the apes but not seen in
    other animals,
The smith, a mighty man, is a personal pronoun
With large and sinuous extremities of his limbs in four
    letters,
And the muscles of his brawny arms
Are as strong as a company of musicians.

Admirable! Isn't it? It only needs a little industry and we can have the whole of our classical literature translated in this way.

But unfortunately the results of the new craze are not always so happy. I heard last week of a rather distressing case of the ill effects of puzzle solving. A man of my acquaintance was at an evening party where they were solving crossword puzzles and he was brought, with the rest of the company, to an absolute full stop by one item: what would you rather be out of than in, in twelve letters? The thing absolutely beat him.

He thought of it all night but with no result. He was still thinking of it as he drove his car down town next morning. In his absolute preoccupation he ran into a man on the street and shook him up quite badly. He was arrested and tried for criminal negligence.

The judge said to him: "I regret very much to have to impose a prison sentence on a man of your standing. But criminal negligence cannot be tolerated. I sentence you to six months in the penitentiary."

On this the puzzle-solver threw up his hands with an exclamation of joy and cried, "Penitentiary, of course, penitentiary! Now I've got it!"

He was scribbling on a little bit of paper when they led him away.

INFORMATION WHILE YOU EAT

Some Reflections on the Joys of the Luncheon Clubs

Now that the bright tints of autumn are appearing on the trees, the season for the luncheon

clubs is opening up again.   Personally I think our
luncheon clubs are one of the most agreeable
features of modern city life.   I have belonged to
several luncheon clubs in our town ever since they
started, and I never miss a lunch.

When I look back to the time when men used
to be satisfied to sit down all alone in front of a
beefsteak and a bottle of Budweiser with only
just some apple pie and a cup of coffee and a
cigar after it, and without singing a note all
through—I don't see how we did it.   Now, if I
can't sing a little as I eat, and call "hear, hear"
every now and then, I don't feel as if I could
digest properly.   So when I offer a few suggestions about our luncheon clubs, I don't want to
be misunderstood.   I am not criticizing but
merely pointing out how we can make them
brighter and better still.

Take the singing.   After all, quite frankly, do
we need to sing at lunch?   Our clubs—and, I
think, the clubs in most other towns, too—generally sing very slow, dragging melodies such as,
"The . . . day . . . is . . . past, . . . the
. . . sun . . . is . . . set. . . ."   The effect
of that kind of tune as intoned by a hundred men

with a pound and a quarter beefsteak adjusted in each of them (125 lbs. total dead-weight of music) is, very frankly mournful. It sounds to me like the last of the Tasmanian Islanders leaving home.

Or else we sing negro melodies. But why should we? Or we sing "Annie Laurie." Who was she, anyway? In fact, to be quite candid, I can eat lunch splendidly without asking to be carried back to Tennessee, or offering to lay down and die, either on the banks of the Doon or anywhere else.

Without the singing there could be a pleasant atmosphere of quiet which is now missing.

Take as another slight point of criticism the chairman's speech, introducing the speaker. There I do think a decided improvement could be made by cutting out the chairman's remarks altogether. They are misleading. He doesn't state things as they are. He always says:

"Today we are to have a rare treat in listening to Mr. Nut. I need not offer any introduction to this audience for a man like Mr. Nut. When we learned that Mr. Nut was to address us, we felt that the club was fortunate indeed."

Now if the man told the truth what he would say would be this:

"Gentlemen, I am sorry to announce that the only speaker we have been able to secure for to-day is this poor simp who is sitting beside me, Mr. Nut. You never heard of him before, gentlemen, but then neither did your committee. But we have hunted everywhere for a speaker, and we simply can't get any except this guy that you see here. He is going to talk to you on 'Our Trade Relations with Nicaragua.'

"I am well aware, gentlemen, that this subject seems utterly without interest. But it appears to be the only subject about which this poor shrimp knows anything. So I won't say any more—I'll let you judge for yourselves what you are going to get. Mr. Nut."

Then, of course, there is the vital question of whether, after all, a luncheon club needs to listen to speeches. Could it not perhaps fulfill its functions just as well if there was no address at all? The trouble is that one never gets time to study up the question beforehand and the recollection that is carried away by what the speaker said is too vague to be of any use.

I will give as an example my own recollection, as far as it goes, of the address that we had at our club last week, to which I have just referred, on the subject of our "Trade Relations with Nicaragua."

Let me say at the start that I am not quite clear whether it was Nicaragua or Nigeria. The chairman seemed to say Nicaragua, but I understood the speaker once or twice to say Nigeria.

I tried to find out afterwards from other members of the club whether it was Nigeria or Nicaragua. But they didn't seem to care. They hear so many people lecture on so many queer places that it runs off them like water. Only a few meetings before they had heard a man talk on "Six Weeks in Bangkok," and right after that another man on "Seven Weeks in Pongo Pongo" and the very next week after that the address was called "Eight Weeks in Itchi-Itchi."

But let it go at Nicaragua, because it is really just about the same. Before the speaker began to say anythng about Nicaragua itself, or Nigeria itself as the case may be, he went through a sort of introduction. All the speakers seem to go over about the same ground in beginning. I tried to write this particular introduction down from memory but I am not sure that I have it correctly. It seemed to run as follows:

"I feel very much honored in being asked to address this club. It is an honor to address this club. And I feel that addressing this club is an honor. When I was invited to address this club I tried to think what I could address this club about. In fact I felt very much like the old darky. This old darky—" Here follows the story of an old darky, which has been told to our club already by six explorers, seven professors, and two clergymen.

It will just about stand repeating in print, but not quite. We always know that when the speaker looks round and say, "There was an old darky—" we are going to get it again. Some of the members can still laugh at it.

But even leaving out the introduction, there are other troubles. The addresses are, no doubt, full of information. But you can't get it. There's too much of it. You can't hold it. Here is what I got, listening as hard as I could, from the address of which I am speaking.

"Probably very few of us realize what a vast

country Nicaragua, or Nigeria, is. It extends from latitude (I didn't catch it) to latitude— I'm not quite sure, and it contains a quarter of a million or half a billion square miles. The principal product is either logwood or dogwood— it may have been deadwood. Sugar either grows excellently or doesn't grow at all—I didn't quite catch which.

The inhabitants are either the mildest or the wildest race known on the globe. They are polygamous and sell their wives freely to travelers for a few glass beads (we all heard that as plainly as anything). The whole of the interior of Nigeria or Nicaragua is dense mud. All that Nicaragua or Nigeria needs is richer soil, a better climate, a decent population, money, civilization, women, and enterprise."

So upon the whole, I am much inclined to doubt whether the speeches are worth while. It is so hard to carry away anything.

And anyway, having speeches means getting too big a crowd. A hundred men is too many. A group of fifty would be far better.

As a matter of fact, a more compact luncheon of, say, twenty would be better still. Twenty men around a table can all converse, they can feel themselves in actual personal contact with one another. With twenty men, or say, fifteen men, you feel you are among a group of friends. In fact, I am not sure but what ten, or eight, would be a cosier crowd still.

You get eight or six men together and you can really exchange ideas. You get a real mental friction with six men that you can't get with a larger number. And moreover with six, or four, men sitting down like this day after day you get to know one another and in point of service and comfort there is no comparison.

You can have a luncheon served for four, or three, men that is really worth eating. As a matter of fact, if it comes to that, two is a better number still.

Indeed the more I think of it the better I like two—myself and a darned good waiter.

THE CHILDREN'S COLUMN

As Brought Up To Date

I suppose that everybody who reads the newspapers is aware of the change that is coming over the thing called the Children's Column, or the Children's Corner, or the Children's Page. Forty years ago it was made up of such things as letters to little boys about how to keep white mice, and letters to little girls about making crochet work in six stitches. But now, what with the radio and progress and the general rapid movement of the age, it is quite different. Here are some samples that are meant to illustrate the change.

ANNO DOMINI 1880

Letter to little Willie Weakhead telling him how to make a Rabbit Hutch:

DEAR WILLIE:

So you want to know how to make a rabbit hutch for your white rabbit? Well, it is not very difficult if you will follow the directions carefully. Get from the nearest joiner a large empty box and some boards about 4 inches wide. (You know what an inch is, do you not?) Then lay the boards across the open side of the box with a space of about two inches between each and nail them in this position. Good nails can be bought in any drugstore but see that you are given ones with good points on them.

If you find it hard to nail on the boards, get your father or your uncle to help you. Be careful in using the hammer not to hit yourself on the thumb, as a blow with a hammer on the thumb is painful and is often followed by a blow on the fingers. Remember, if it starts to rain while you are working on your hutch, come in out of the wet.

Let us know how you get on and whether your bunnies like their new home.

Your's etc.

UNCLE TOBY (Editor: Children's Column)

But contrast with this the modern thing which in these days of radio and modern science has taken the place of the rabbit hutch correspondence.

ANNO DOMINI 1926

Letter from the Editor to Little Willie Wisebean, grandson of the above, in regard to the difficulties which he is finding with his radio apparatus.

DEAR WILLIE:

You write that the other night in attempting to call up Arizona KQW on your radio, you found an inordinate amount of static on your antennae. We quite agree with you that the trouble was perhaps due to purely atmospheric conditions causing a fall in the potential. You can easily find out if this is the case by calculating the differential wave length shown by your variometer.

As you rightly say your apparatus may have been put out of order by your allowing your father and your grandfather into your workshop. If you are wise you will keep them out. As you say yourself, they are too old to learn and they may meet some injury in handling your machine. You say that your grandfather used to be very fond of carpentry and once made a rabbit hutch. Why not let him set to work now and make a rabbit hutch to put your father in?

By the way, if it turns out that your trouble is in your magnetic coils, we advise you not to try to remedy them but to buy new ones. You can get excellent coils from Messers. Grabb and Gettit, for $100 a coil, or even more. On this

your father might come in useful.   With thanks
for your interesting letter,

> PROFESSOR I. KNOWIT, Ph.D. T.K., D.F.
> Oxon; Harvard, Oklahoma.

Or let us turn to another part of the same
field—the feminine side.   The change is even
more striking.   Compare the two following letters to the Lady Editor, making enquiries in each
case about the way to arrange a children's party
for little girls.

ANNO DOMINI 1880

*Letter to Dollie Dollhouse, aged 14, who has
asked for advice about a party.*

DEAR DOLLIE:

I am so glad to hear that you are going to give
a party to your little girl friends for your four-
teenth birthday.   Of course you must have straw-
berries, great big luscious ones with lots of cream
all over them.   And of course you must have
a lovely big cake, with icing all over the top of
it, and you must put fourteen candles on it.   Do
you see the idea of the candles, dear?   No, per-

haps not at first, but if you will think a minute
you will see it. It means that you are fourteen
years old and that there is a candle for every
year. Isn't it a pretty thought, once you understand it? I got it out of an old Norwegian
book of fairy stories and thought it so sweet.

You had better not try to light the candles
yourself, but get your papa or your mama to
come and do it, if they do not like to, then send
for a man from the hardware store.

You say that after all the girls have eaten
all they can you would like to have some games
and ask what you can play. There are really
such a lot of games that it is hard to advise,
but among the best of the new games is one
called *Hunt the Slipper,* which I am sure you
would like. All that you need for playing it
with is an old slipper, one without any tacks
sticking out of it being the best. One of the
girls sits on the slipper and then the player who
is chosen to begin has to go round and roll over
all the girls and see where the slipper is. You
see it is quite a clever game and can easily be
learned in half an hour. But remember that
your play must never be rough. In rolling over

the girls pick them up by the feet and roll them over in a ladylike way.

After the game if you can get your papa to come into the room and read a selection of poetry, such as a couple of cantos from *Paradise Lost,* the girls will go away delighted.

With best love and good wishes for your party,

· AUNT AGATHA
Lady Editor Children's Column.

Here is the other sample which is the same thing, brought up to date.

ANNO DOMINI 1926

Letter to Flossie Fitz Clippit, aged 14, granddaughter of Dollie Dollhouse, in answer to her request for advice about a party.

DEAR FLOSSIE:

The right number of covers for a luncheon to your girl friends is certainly eight. Ten, as you yourself seem to think, is too large a number to be cosy, while eight gives exactly the feeling of *cameraderie* without too much formality. Six, on the other hand, is a little too *intime,* while seven rather carries the idea of oddity, of something a little *louche,* or at least *gauche,* if not *hootch.*

For table decorations I find it hard to advise you, as I do not know the tinting of your room, nor the draperies or the shape and shade of your table and the complexion of your butler. But if not unsuitable for some special reason what do you say to great bunches of scarlet ilex thrown all over the table? Either that or large masses of wisteria and big bunches of Timothy hay?

I don't think that if I were you I would serve cocktails before lunch, as some of your friends might have views about it, but a delicious *coupe* can be made by mixing half a bottle of old rum with shredded wheat and then soaking it in gin.

For the menu, you will want something light and dainty, appealing rather by its exquisite taste than by sheer quantity. What do you say to beginning with a *canapé* of *paté de fois gras,* followed by a *purée* of mushrooms and leading up to a broiled lobster followed by a porterhouse beefsteak. I think that is the kind of thing that your little friends would like. And if you have after it a *soufflé,* and a few quarts of ice cream with angel cake it will be found quite enough.

I quite sympathize with what you say about not wanting your mother. There is no doubt that the presence of a mother at any kind of entertainment gives a touch of coldness, a lack of affection. Your father, of course, is quite impossible; though I think it would be all right to let him shake hands with the girls as they pass out. At a recent luncheon where I was present I saw both the father and the mother brought into the drawing room for a few moments and introduced to the guests. The effect was really very sweet, with quite an old world touch to it. But I would not try to imitate it if I were you. Better be content with having the butler take up half a gallon of the *coupe* to your father in his library.

You will of course want to know about cigarettes. I should particularly recommend the new Egyptian *Dingos,* or, if you have not yet tried them, the new Peruvian *Guanos*. They seem to be the last word in tobacco.

With regards and good wishes,
Man-Lady Editor Children's
Adult Column.

OLD PROVERBS MADE NEW

It has occurred to me that somebody in one
of the English departments of our colleges ought
to get busy and re-write our national proverbs.
They are all out of date. They don't fit any
longer. Indeed, many of them are precisely the
converse of existing facts.

Our proverbs have come down to us from the
days of long ago; days when the world was very
primitive and very simple and very different;
when people never moved more than a mile and
a half from home and were all afraid of the
dark; and when wisdom was handed out by old
men with white whiskers called *prophets,* every
one of whom would be "retired" nowadays by
any first class board of trustees as past the age-
limit of common sense.

But in those days all the things that were said
by these wise old men, who had never seen a
motor car, were gathered up and called proverbs
and repeated by all the common people as the
last words of wisdom. The result is that even
today we still go on repeating them, without re-
alizing how hopelessly they are off the track.

Take as a first sample the proverb that is perhaps the best known in our language:

BIRDS OF A FEATHER FLOCK TOGETHER

But they don't. Ask any first class naturalist. If the wise old men had taken another look they would have seen that the last thing birds ever want to do is to flock together. In ninety-nine cases out of a hundred they keep away from their own species, and only flock when it is absolutely necessary. So much for the birds. But the proverb is really supposed to refer to people and then it is wrong again. People "of a feather" do not flock together. Tall men fall in love with little women. A girl with a beautiful fair skin and red hair marries a man who looks like a reformed orang-outang. A clergyman makes a friend of an auctioneer and a banker would rather spend a day with an Adirondack fishing guide than with a whole vaultful of bankers. Burglars during the daytime go and swim in the Y. M. C. A. pool. Forgers in their off time sing in the

choir, and choirmasters when they are not singing shoot craps.

In short, there is nothing in the proverb what-
soever. It ought to be revised under the modern
conditions to read:

Birds of any particular feather and persons of
any particular character or occupation show upon
the whole a disposition rather to seek out some-
thing dissimilar to their own appearance and
nature than to consort with something homo-
logous to their own essential entity.

In that shape one has a neat workable proverb.
Try another:

A ROLLING STONE GATHERS NO MOSS

Entirely wrong again. This was supposed to
show that a young man who wandered from
home never got on in the world. In very ancient
days it was true. The young man who stayed
at home and worked hard and tilled the ground
and goaded oxen with a long stick like a lance
found himself as he grew old a man of property,
owning four goats and a sow. The son who
wandered forth in the world was either killed by

the cannibals or crawled home years afterwards doubled up with rheumatism. So the old men made the proverb. But nowadays it is exactly wrong. It is the rolling stone that gathers the moss. It is the ambitious boy from Honkville, Indiana, who trudges off to the city leaving his elder brother in the barnyard and who later makes a fortune and founds a university. While his elder brother still has only the old farm with three cows and a couple of pigs, he has a whole department of agriculture with great sheds-full of Tamworth hogs and a professor to every six of them.

In short, in modern life it is the rolling stone that gathers the moss. And the geologists— outside of Tennessee—say that the moss on the actual stone was first started in exactly the same way. It was the rolling of the stone that smashed up the earth and made the moss grow.

Take another proverb:

ALL IS NOT GOLD THAT GLITTERS

How perfectly ridiculous! Everybody in the days in which we live knows—even a child knows—that all *is* gold that glitters. Put on clothes enough, appearance enough and you will be accepted anywhere. Just do a little glittering and everybody will think you are gold. Make a show, be a humbug, and you will succeed so fast that presently, being very wealthy and prominent, you will really think yourself a person of great merit and intellect. In other words, the glitter makes the gold. That is all there *is* to it. Gold is really one of the most useless of all material objects. Even now we have found no *real* use for it, except to fill our teeth. Any other employment of it is just *glitter*. So the proverb might be revised to read:

Every thing or person may be said to stand in high esteem and to pass at a high value provided that it or he makes a sufficient show, glitter, or appearance, the estimation being in inverse ratio to the true quantitative measurement of the reality of it, them or her. That makes a neat workable proverb, expressed with up-to-date accuracy.

Or here is another famous proverb that is exactly the contrary of truth:

PEOPLE WHO LIVE IN GLASS HOUSES OUGHT NOT TO THROW STONES

Not at all. They are the very people who ought to throw stones and to keep on throwing them all the time. They ought to keep up such a fusillade of stones from their glass house that no one can get near it.

Or if the proverb is taken to mean that people who have faults of their own ought not to talk of other people's faults, it is equally mistaken. They ought to talk of other people's faults all the time so as to keep attention away from their own.

But the list of proverbs is so long that it is impossible to do more than make a casual mention of a few others.

ONE SWALLOW DOES NOT MAKE A SUMMER. Perhaps not. But there are ever so many occasions when one swallow,—just one single swallow—is better than nothing to drink at all. And if you get enough of them they *do* make a summer.

CHARITY BEGINS AT HOME. Perfectly ridiculous. Watch any modern city householder when a beggar comes to his door. Charity begins with the Federated Charities Office, or with the Out of Work Mission, or with the City Hall, or if need be, with the Police Court—in short, *anywhere* but at home. Our whole effort is now to keep charity as far from home as possible.

IT IS A WISE CHILD THAT KNOWS ITS OWN FATHER. Not at all. Alter this and make it read: It is a very silly boy who isn't on to his old man.

EVEN A WORM WILL TURN AT LAST. Wrong. It turns at once, immediately. It never waits.

A BIRD IN THE HAND IS WORTH TWO IN THE BUSH. Yes, but a bird in a good restaurant is worth ten of either of them.

There—that's enough. Any reader of this book may go on having fun with the other proverbs. I give them to him.

125

IV
IN THE GOOD OLD
SUMMER TIME

The Merry Month of May

As Treated in the Bye-Gone Almanacs

THE part of the year known in ballad poetry as the Good Old Summer Time begins with what is popularly called the Merry Month of May. The winter is then over except in the city of Quebec, in Butte, Montana, and in the Back Bay regions of Boston. The gathering warmth of the sun calls all nature to life.

The Heavens in May

In the older almanacs of the kind that used to be made for farmers, the first items under this month always dealt with the aspect of the heavens. The farmer was told that in May the sun, passing out of the sign of Taurus, moved into the constellation of Gemini; that the apparent declination of the sun was 15 degrees and 4 minutes and that the neap tides fell on the thirteenth and twenty-seventh of the month. He was also informed that Mars and Mercury during May are both in opposition and that Sirius is the dog star.

In the city this information is now useless. Nobody can see the heavens even if he wants to; the open space between the skyscrapers formerly called the sky is now filled with electric lights, pictures of motor wheels turning round, and men eating breakfast food with a moving spoon.

We doubt also if the up-to-date farmer is really concerned with the Zodiac. We will therefore only say that in this month if the farmer will on any clear night ascend to the cupola of his pergola with his binoculars and with his radio plugs in his ears and his insulators on his feet and view the heavens from midnight till three in the morning, he will run a first class chance of getting pneumonia.

The Garden in May

For those to whom gardening—even in the limited restrictions of a city back yard—is a hobby and a passion, the month of May is the most enticing month of the year. It seems strange to think that so many men with a back yard at their disposal—a back yard let us say, twenty feet by fifteen—should nevertheless spend the long evenings and the Saturday afternoons of the month of May striding up and down the golf links or wandering along a trout stream. How much better to be out in the back yard with a spade and hoe, pickaxe and sledge hammer and a little dynamite preparing the exuberant soil for the luxuriant crop.

In the amateur garden in the back yard no great technical knowledge is needed. Our citizen gardener who wishes to begin should go out into his back yard and having stripped himself to his waist, all but his undershirt, should proceed first to dig out his ground.

He must excavate a hole ten by fifteen, by ten by two; of course, the hole won't be as big as that, but it will *seem* to be. He must carefully remove on his back all large boulders, volcanic rocks, and other accumulated debris. These if he likes he may fashion tastefully into a rockery or a rookery, or also, if he likes, he may throw them over the fence into his neighbor's back yard. He must then proceed to fill the hole half full of sweet-smelling fertilizer.

This will almost complete his first evening's work. In fact, he will be just about filling in his stuff when the other men come past on their way home from golf. He will then finish his task by putting back a fourth of the soil, which he will carefully pulverize by lying down and rolling in it. After this he can then take a bath (or two baths) and go to bed.

The ground thus carefully prepared, the amateur gardener should wait a day or so and then, proceeding to his back yard, should draw on his overalls up to his neck and proceed to plant his bulbs and seeds.

The tulip is a favorite flower for early planting owing to its fine raucous appearance. Excellent tulip bulbs may be had of any florist for one dollar, which with proper care will turn into a flower worth thirty cents. The dahlia, the most handsome of the ganglions, almost repays cultivation, presenting a splendid carboniferous appearance with unsurpassed efflorescence. The potato is not bad, either.

The Merry Month of May

When the garden plot is all filled up with buried bulbs and seeds, the gardener should roll the dirt down flat, by rolling it, and then for the rest of the month of May, sit and look at it.

A Cool Drink for May

The month of May is the time of year when dandelion wine, owing to the presence of dandelions, is perhaps easier to make than at any other time. An excellent recipe is as follows:

1. Pluck, or pick, a small basketful of dandelion heads.
2. Add to them a quart of water and leave the mixture to stand for five minutes.
3. Pour off the water, remove the dandelions, and add as flavoring a quart of 1872 champagne.
4. Drink it.

The Countryside in May

It is in the month of May that the countryside, for the true lover of nature, is at its best. For one who knows by name and can distinguish and classify the flora of the lanes and fields, a country walk among the opening buds is a scene of unalloyed joy. The tiny hibiscus is seen peeping out from under the grass while everywhere in the spring air is the sweet scent of the ornithorhyncus and the megalotherium. One should watch in this month for the first shoots of the spiggot, while the trained eye will easily distinguish the lambswart, the dogsfoot, and the cowslip.

Nor are the birds, for anyone who knows their names, less interesting than the flowers. The corvex americanus is building its nest in the tall timber. The sharp whistling notes of the ilex and the pulex and the index are heard in the meadows, while the marshes are loud with the song of the ranunculus. But of course for those who do not know these names nothing is happening except that a lot of birds are singing and the grass is growing. That, of course, is quite worthless and uninteresting.

Great Events in May

May 1. Birth of Shakespeare.
May 5. End of the Trojan war.
May 10. Beginning of the Trojan war.

May 15.   Birth of Shakespeare.

May 20.   Shakespeare born.

May 25.   Trojan war ends again.

May 30.   Death of Shakespeare and beginning of the Trojan war.

HOW WE KEPT MOTHER'S BIRTHDAY

As Related by a Member of the Family

Of all the different ideas that have been started lately, I think that the very best is the notion of celebrating once a year "Mother's Day." I don't wonder that May the eleventh is becoming such a popular date all over America and I am sure the idea will spread to England too.

It is especially in a big family like ours that such an idea takes hold. So we decided to have a special celebration of Mother's Day. We thought it a fine idea. It made us all realize how much Mother had done for us for years, and all the efforts and sacrifice that she had made for our sake.

135

So we decided that we'd make it a great day, a holiday for all the family, and do everything we could to make Mother happy. Father decided to take a holiday from his office, so as to help in celebrating the day, and my sister Anne and I stayed home from college classes, and Mary and my brother Will stayed home from High School.

It was our plan to make it a day just like Xmas or any big holiday, and so we decided to decorate the house with flowers and with mottoes over the mantelpieces, and all that kind of thing. We got Mother to make mottoes and arrange the decorations, because she always does it at Xmas.

The two girls thought it would be a nice thing to dress in our very best for such a big occasion, and so they both got new hats. Mother trimmed both the hats, and they looked fine, and Father had bought four-in-hand silk ties for himself and us boys as a souvenir of the day to remember Mother by. We were going to get Mother a new hat too, but it turned out that she seemed to really like her old grey bonnet better than a new one, and both the girls said that it was awfully becoming to her.

Well, after breakfast we had it arranged as a surprise for Mother that we would hire a motor car and take her for a beautiful drive away into the country. Mother is hardly ever able to have a treat like that, because we can only afford to keep one maid, and so Mother is busy in the house nearly all the time. And of course the country is so lovely now that it would be just grand for her to have a lovely morning, driving for miles and miles.

But on the very morning of the day we changed the plan a little bit, because it occurred to Father that a thing it would be better to do even than to take Mother for a motor drive would be to take her fishing. Father said that as the car was hired and paid for, we might just as well use it for a drive up into hills where the streams are. As Father said, if you just go out driving without any object, you have a sense of aimlessness, but if you are going to fish, there is a definite purpose in front of you to heighten the enjoyment.

So we all felt that it would be nicer for Mother

137

to have a definite purpose; and anyway, it turned out that Father had just got a new rod the day before, which made the idea of fishing all the more appropriate, and he said that Mother could use it if she wanted to; in fact, he said it was practically for her, only Mother said she would much rather watch him fish and not to try to fish herself.

So we got everything arranged for the trip, and we got Mother to cut up some sandwiches and make up a sort of lunch in case we got hungry, though of course we were to come back home again to a big dinner in the middle of the day, just like Xmas or New Year's Day. Mother packed it all up in a basket for us ready to go in the motor.

Well, when the car came to the door, it turned out that there hardly seemed as much room in it as we had supposed, because we hadn't reckoned on Father's fishing basket and the rods and the lunch, and it was plain enough that we couldn't all get in.

Father said not to mind him, he said that he could just as well stay home, and that he was sure that he could put in the time working in the garden; he said that there was a lot of rough dirty work that he could do, like digging a trench for the garbage, that would save hiring a man, and so he said that he'd stay home; he said that we were not to let the fact of his not having had a real holiday for three years stand in our way; he wanted us to go right ahead and be happy and have a big day, and not to mind him. He said that he could plug away all day, and in fact he said he'd been a fool to think there'd be any holiday for him.

But of course we all felt that it would never do to let Father stay home, especially as we knew he would make trouble if he did. The two girls Anna and Mary, would gladly have stayed and helped the maid get dinner, only it seemed such a pity to, on a lovely day like this, having their new hats. But they both said that Mother had only to say the word, and they'd gladly stay home and work. Will and I would have dropped out, but unfortunately we wouldn't have been any use in getting the dinner.

So in the end it was decided that Mother would stay home and just have a lovely restful day round the house, and get the dinner. It turned out anyway that Mother doesn't care for fishing, and also it was just a little bit cold and fresh out of doors, though it was lovely and sunny, and Father was rather afraid that Mother might take cold if she came.

He said he would never forgive himself if he dragged Mother round the country and let her take a severe cold at a time when she might be having a beautiful rest. He said it was our duty to try and let Mother get all the rest and quiet that she could, after all that she had done for all of us, and he said that that was principally why he had fallen in with this idea of a fishing trip, so as to give Mother a little quiet. He said that young people seldom realize how much quiet means to people who are getting old. As to himself, he could still stand the racket, but he was glad to shelter Mother from it.

So we all drove away with three cheers for Mother, and Mother stood and watched us from the verandah for as long as she could see us, and Father waved his hand back to her every few minutes till he hit his hand on the back edge of the car, and then said that he didn't think that Mother could see us any longer.

Well,—we had the loveliest day up among the hills that you could possibly imagine, and Father caught such big specimens that he felt sure that Mother couldn't have landed them anyway, if she had been fishing for them, and Will and I fished too, though we didn't get so many as Father, and the two girls met quite a lot of people that they knew as we drove along, and there were some young men friends of theirs that they met along the stream and talked to, and so we all had a splendid time.

It was quite late when we got back, nearly seven o'clock in the evening, but Mother had guessed that we would be late, so she had kept back the dinner so as to have it just nicely ready and hot for us. Only first she had to get towels and soap for Father and clean things for him to put on, because he always gets so messed up with fishing, and that kept Mother busy for a little while, that and helping the girls get ready.

But at last everything was ready, and we sat down to the grandest kind of dinner—roast turkey and all sorts of things like on Xmas Day. Mother had to get up and down a good bit during the meal fetching things back and forward, but at the end Father noticed it and said she simply mustn't do it, that he wanted her to spare herself, and he got up and fetched the walnuts over from the sideboard himself.

The dinner lasted a long while, and was great fun, and when it was over all of us wanted to help clear the things up and wash the dishes, only Mother said that she would really much rather do it, and so we let her, because we wanted just for once to humor her.

It was quite late when it was all over, and when we all kissed Mother before going to bed, she said it had been the most wonderful day in her life, and I think there were tears in her eyes. So we all felt awfully repaid for all that we had done.

SUMMER SORROWS OF THE SUPER-RICH

In the course of each summer it is my privilege to do some visiting in the class of the super-rich. By this I mean the class of people who have huge estates at such fashionable places as Nagahucket, and Dogblastit, and up near Lake Owatawetness, where the country is so beautifully wild that it costs a thousand dollars an acre.

Even people who had never had the opportunity of moving about away up in this class know more or less the sort of establishment I mean. When you visit one of these houses you always pass a "lodge" with a bright bed of flowers in front of it, which is a sign that the house itself is now only three miles away.

Later on the symptoms begin to multiply. You see a log cabin summer-house made to imitate a settler's home and built out of cedar imported from the Fiji Islands. Then presently there is a dear little waterfall and a dam of great slabs of rock, built for only a hundred and fifty thousand dollars and supplying electric light worth forty cents an evening.

After that you pass Scotch gardeners planting out little fir trees and go through a zone of woodsmen cutting birch billets for open fires, and chauffeurs, resting, and there you are all of a sudden in front of Dogblastit House, standing beside

143

its own lake, with its own mountains and ten
thousand acres of the finest natural woods ever
staged by landscape gardeners.

Now would you think that the people who
live in these great places are happy? They are
not. They have troubles of which you and I
and the ordinary people never dream. They
come out to the wilderness to rough it, and to
snatch a brief four months' vacation between the
strain of the Riviera and the pressure of New
York, and then right in the happiest season of
the summer, they come up against desperate
problems.

The particular ones that follow were related
to me at Dogblastit. But I gather that the same
difficulties are met in all establishments of the
sort. They are discussed in all the conversation
among hosts and guests, just as we discussed them
last summer around the birch fires in the lounge
at Dogblastit.

PROBLEM NO. 1. *What to do to amuse
the butler in the evening?* It seems that he
doesn't play bridge. The butler who was here
last year was always quite content if he could
be provided with a game of bridge, and except

for a run to New York now and then and a trip to see his brother in Vancouver in the middle of the summer, he stayed on the place without a break and seemed quite satisfied.

But the new man Jennings doesn't care for cards. He says quite frankly that it is not a matter of conscience and that he doesn't mind cards in the house, but they simply don't interest him. So what can one do?

PROBLEM NO. 2. *How to get the chauffeur's collars starched?* It appears that there have been very great difficulties at Dogblastit about this. It is very hard to get the kind of gloss that Ransome likes on his collars. There is, of course, an electric laundry in the basement of Dogblastit itself, but unfortunately the laundry maids who do the work in it will not undertake any collars over eleven inches long. They say they simply won't undertake them.

The experiment was made of bringing up a laundress from Boston, but it was found that she wouldn't undertake to starch anything at such a high altitude. She can only do her work at from 500 to 800 feet above the sea. Beyond that, she said, she could do nothing.

They tried also sending Ransome's collars by express to New York, but this was quite unsatisfactory, because the express people threw them about so roughly. More than once they were seen actually throwing the packet of Ransome's collars right from the platform of Dogblastit station into the express car. The only feasible thing up to now has been to have Ransome take one of the cars and drive his collars either to New York or to Philadelphia. The objection is that it takes up so much of his time, especially as he always likes to drive his boots over to Burlington, Vermont, once a week, where he can get them properly treated.

PROBLEM NO. 3. *What to get for the cook to read on Sunday?* The trouble is, she doesn't care for fiction. She evidently is a woman of literary culture, because she said one day that she had read the whole of Shakespeare and thought it very good. In the library of Dogblastit itself, which is a really beautiful room done in Japanese oak with leaded windows to represent the reading room of a settler's cabin, there are practically no books that suit the cook. In fact, there is nothing but the Blue Book (one

needs that to look up people in) and the Pink
Book and the Red Book, and of course the Auto-
mobile Road Book and then some Guide Books
such as *The Perfect Bartender,* and the *Gentleman's Cellar* and *Cocktails for all Occasions.*

Beyond that there are, of course, all the new
books—the new fiction—because there is a standing order with Spentano to send up fifty pounds
of new fiction by express once a week. None of
the guests of the house ever care to read any
book more than three weeks old, as they are
quite worthless for conversation.

An order was sent to Boston for the Harvard
Classics but the cook says she doesn't care for
the way they are selected. The only com-
promise so far is to get her books about the South
Seas. She says she is just crazy over the South
Sea literature. So we have given her *Six Weeks
in the Marquesas Islands* and *Four days in
Fiji, Half Hours in Hoo-Poo.* But all that will
only last her less than seven weeks, and after
that we don't know what to do.

PROBLEM NO. 4. *What to do with the
governess when she is not working?* This has
proved up to the present a quite insoluble prob-

lem. It is so hard to know just what to do with Mademoiselle after she has finished governing the children. We can't, so it is felt, have her in the drawing room and yet what can one do with her? We have tried shutting her up in the garage, but that is dull. In open weather we can lock her out on the piazza, but she is apt to get from there into the billiard room where the guests are. The only plan seems to be to give her somewhere a cosy, little wee room for herself, either at the back of the ash-house, or else underneath the laundry.

The problems I have named are the principal ones—the ones that always recur in any large house of real class and standing. But there are a lot of others as well that I need not treat in detail. For example, there is the difficult question of how to keep Robert, the under-gardener, out of the kitchen. Robert would never have been engaged if it had been known that he was a dangerous man. But this was only reported by the house-keeper after Robert had been brought up and had been in the house a week. When you bring a man up you can't bring him down.

And who is it that is stealing all the jewelry? We don't like to make any fuss or disturbance. But another diamond ring went last night and one feels that something ought to be done.

My visits with my fashionable friends have been so much disturbed by perpetual conversation on these problems that I have decided to give them up altogether and to get back into my own class of society. I have some friends, real ones, who have a wooden house on an island where there is no electric light within twenty miles and where they use rainwater out of a barrel.

They have coal-oil lanterns to see by; they wear flannel collars and they pass the soap from one room to another as it is needed. The men cut the firewood, as required, and never keep more than half an hour's supply on hand, and the girls do all the work because help can't be got and they know ten different ways of cooking canned salmon.

I am going back there. For me that is the only real old summer stuff that is worth while. I was brought up on it and have never grown out of it. Anybody who likes may have my room and my tiled bath at Dogblastit.

HOW MY WIFE AND I BUILT OUR HOME FOR $4.90

Related in the Manner of the Best Models in the Magazines

I was leaning up against the mantelpiece in a lounge suit which I had made out of old ice bags, and Beryl, my wife, was seated at my feet on a low Louis Quinze tabouret which she had made out of a Finnan Haddie fishbox, when the idea of a bungalow came to both of us at the same time.

"It would be just lovely if we could do it!" exclaimed Beryl, coiling herself around my knee.

"Why not!" I replied, lifting her up a little by the ear. "With your exquisite taste,——"

"And with your knowledge of material," added Beryl, giving me a tiny pinch on the leg— "Oh, I am sure we could do it! One reads so much in all the magazines about people making summer bungalows and furnishing them for next to nothing. Oh, do let us try, Dogyard!"

We talked over our project all night, and the next morning we sallied forth to try to find a site

for our new home. As Beryl (who was brim-
ming over with fun as the result of talking all
night) put it, "The first thing is to get the
ground."

Here fortune favored us. We had hardly
got to the edge of the town when Beryl suddenly
exclaimed, "Oh look, Dogyard, look, there's exactly the site!" It was a piece of waste land on
the edge of a gully with a brickyard on one side
of it and a gravel pit on the other. It had no
trees on it, and it was covered with ragged heaps
of tin cans, old newspapers, and stones, and a
litter of broken lumber.

Beryl's quick eye saw the possibilities of the
situation at once. "Oh, Dogyard!" she exclaimed, "isn't it just sweet? We can clear away
all this litter and plant a catalpa tree to hide the
brickyard and a hedge of copernicus or nux vom-
ica to hide the gravel pit, and some bright flowers
to hide the hedge. I wish I had brought some
catalpa seed. They grow so quickly."

"We'd better at least wait," I said, "till we
have bought the ground."

And here a sudden piece of good fortune
awaited us. It so happened that the owner of

151

the lot was on the spot at the time—he was seated on a stone whittling a stick while we were talking, and presented himself to us. After a short discussion he agreed to sell us the ground for one dollar in cash and fifty cents on a three years' mortgage. The deed of sale was written out on the spot and stamped with a two-cent stamp, and the owner of the lot took his departure with every expression of good will. And the magic sense of being owners of our own ground rendered us both jubilant.

That evening Beryl, seated on her little stool at my feet, took a pencil and paper and set down triumphantly a statement of the cost of our bungalow up to date. I introduce it here as a help to readers who may hope to follow in our footsteps:

```
Ground site ................,........$1.50
Stamp for mortgage .............   .02
Car fare ......................   .10
                                 ————
            Total ........$1.62
```

I checked over Beryl's arithmetic twice and found it strictly correct.

Next morning we commenced work in earnest. While Beryl cleared away the cans and litter, I set to work with spade and shovel excavating our cellar and digging out the foundations. And here I must admit that I had no light task. I can only warn those who wish to follow in our footsteps that they must be prepared to face hard work.

Owing perhaps to my inexperience, it took me the whole of the morning to dig out a cellar forty feet long and twenty feet wide. Beryl, who had meantime cleaned up the lot, stacked the lumber, lifted away the stones and planted fifty yards of hedge, was inclined to be a little impatient. But I reminded her that a contractor working with a gang of men and two or three teams of horses would have taken a whole week to do what I did in one morning.

I admitted that my work was not equal to the best records as related in the weekly home journals, where I have often computed that they move 100,000 cubic feet of earth in one paragraph, but at least I was doing my best. Beryl, whose disappointment never lasts, was all smiles again in a moment, and rewarded me by throwing herself around my neck and giving me a hug.

That afternoon I gathered up all the big stones and built them into walls around the cellar with partition walls across it, dividing it into rooms and compartments. I leveled the floor and packed it tight with sand and gravel and dug a drain ten feet deep from the cellar to the gully about thirty feet away.

There being still a good hour or so of daylight left, I dug a cistern four feet wide and twenty feet deep. I was looking round for something more to dig by moonlight, but Beryl put her foot down (on my head while I was in the drain) and forbade me to work any more for fear I might be fatigued.

Next morning we were able to begin our building in good earnest. On our way we stopped at the fifteen cent store for necessary supplies, and bought one hammer, fifteen cents; a saw, fifteen cents; half a gallon of nails, fifteen cents; a crane, fifteen cents; a derrick for hoisting, fifteen cents, and a needle and thread, for sewing on the roof, fifteen cents.

As an advice to young builders, I may say that I doubt if we were quite wise in all our purchases.

The fifteen cent derrick is too light for the work, and the extra expenditure for the heavier kind (the twenty-five cent crane) would have been justified. The difference in cost is only (approximately) ten cents, and the efficiency of the big crane is far greater.

On arriving at our ground we were delighted to find that our masonry was well set and the walls firm and solid, while the catalpa trees were well above the ground and growing rapidly. We set to work at once to build in earnest.

We had already decided to utilize for our bungalow the waste material which lay on our lot. I drew Beryl's attention to the fact that if a proper use were made of the material wasted in building there would be no need to buy any material at all. "The elimination of waste," I explained, "by the utilization of all by-products before they have time to go by, is the central principle of modern industrial organization."

But observing that Beryl had ceased to listen to me, I drew on my carpenter's apron which I had made out of a piece of tar-paper, and set to work. My first care was to gather up all the loose lumber that lay upon and around our ground site, and saw it up into neatly squared pieces about twenty feet long. Out of these I made the joists, the studding, the partitions, rafters, and so on, which formed the frame of the house.

Putting up the house took practically the whole morning. Beryl, who had slipped on a potato bag over her dress, assisted me by holding up the side of the house while I nailed on the top.

By the end of the afternoon we had completed the sides of our house, which we made out of old newspaper soaked in glue and rolled flat. The next day we put on the roof, which was made of tin cans cut open and pounded flat.

For our hardwood floors, mantels, etc., we were fortunate in finding a pile of hardwood on a neighboring lot which had apparently been overlooked, and which we carried over proudly to our bungalow after dark. That same night we carried over jubilantly some rustic furniture which we had found, quite neglected, lying in a nearby cottage, the lock of which oddly enough, was opened quite easily with the key of Beryl's suitcase.

The rest of our furniture—plain tables, dressers, etc.—I was able to make from ordinary pine lumber which I obtained by knocking down a board fence upon an adjacent lot. In short, the reader is able to picture our bungalow after a week of labor, complete in every respect and only awaiting our occupation on the next day.

Seated that evening in our boarding house, with Beryl coiled around me, I calculated the entire cost of our enterprise,—including ground site, lumber, derricks, cranes, glue, string, tin-tacks and other materials—as four dollars and ninety cents.

In return for it we had a pretty seven-roomed house, artistic in every respect, with living-room, bed-rooms, a boudoir, a den, a snuggery, a doggery—in short, the bungalow of which so many young people have dreamed.

Seated together that evening, Beryl and I were full of plans for the future. We both have a passionate love of animals and, like all country-bred people, a longing for the life of a farm. So we had long since decided to keep poultry. We planned to begin in a small way, and had brought home that evening from the fifteen-cent store a day-old chicken, such as are now so widely sold.

We put him in a basket beside the radiator in a little flannel coat that Beryl had made for him, and we fed him with a warm mash made of breakfast food and gravel. Our printed directions that we got with him told us that a fowl eats two ounces of grain per day and on that should lay five eggs in a week. I was easily able to prove to Beryl by a little plain arithmetic that if we fed this fellow 4 ounces a day he would lay 10 eggs in a week, or at 8 ounces per day he would lay 20 eggs in a week.

Beryl, who was seized at once with a characteristic fit of enthusiasm, suggested that we stick 16 ounces a day into him and begin right now. I had to remind her laughingly that at 8 ounces a day the fellow would probably be working up to a capacity, and carrying what we call in business his peak load. "The essential factor in modern business," I told her, "is to load yourself up to the peak and stay there."

In short, there was no end to our rosy dreams. In our fancy we saw ourselves in our bungalow, surrounded by hens, bees, cows and dogs, with hogs and goats nestling against our feet. Unfortunately our dreams were destined to be shattered. Up to this point our experience with building our bungalow had followed along after all the best models, and had even eclipsed them. But from now on we met a series of disasters of which we had had no warning. It is a pity that I cannot leave our story at this point.

On arriving at our bungalow next day we found notices posted up forbidding all trespassers, and two sour-looking men in possession. We learned that our title to the ground site was worthless, as the man from whom we had bought it had been apparently a mere passer-by. It appeared also that a neighboring contractor was making serious difficulties about our use of his material. It was divulged further that we had been mistaken in thinking that we had taken our rustic furniture from an empty cottage. There were people living in it, but they happened to be asleep when Beryl moved the furniture.

As for our hen—there is no doubt that keeping fowls is enormously profitable. It must be so, when one considers the millions of eggs consumed every day. But it demands an unremitting attention and above all—memory. If you own a hen you must never forget it—you must keep on saying to yourself— "How is my hen?" This was our trouble. Beryl and I were so preoccupied with our accumulated disaster, that we left our one-day-old chick behind the radiator and never thought of him for three weeks. He was then gone. We prefer to think that he flew away.

THE EVERLASTING ANGLER

The fishing season is now well under way. Will soon be with us. For lovers of fishing this remark is true all the year round. It has seemed to me that it might be of use to set down a few of the more familiar fish stories that are needed by any one wanting to qualify as an angler. There is no copyright on these stories, since Methuselah first told them, and anybody who wishes may learn them by heart and make free use of them.

I will begin with the simplest and best known. Everybody who goes fishing has heard it, and told it a thousand times. It is called:——

I

THE STORY OF THE FISH THAT WAS LOST

The circumstances under which the story is best told are these. The fisherman returns after his day's outing with his two friends whom he has taken out for the day, to his summer cottage. They carry with them their rods, their landing net and the paraphernalia of their profession. The fisherman carries also on a string a dirty looking collection of little fish, called by courtesy the "Catch." None of these little fish really measures more than about seven and a half inches long and four inches round the chest. The fisherman's wife and his wife's sister and the young lady who is staying with them come running to meet the fishing party, giving cries of admiration as they get a sight of the catch. In reality they would refuse to buy those fish from a butcher at a cent and a half a pound. But they fall into ecstasies and they cry, "Oh aren't they beauties! Look at this big one!" The "big one" is about eight inches long. It looked good when they caught it but it has been shrinking ever since and it looks now as if it had died of consumption. Then it is that the fisherman says, in a voice in which regret is mingled with animation:

"Yes, but say, you ought to have seen the one that we lost. We had hardly let down our lines——"

It may be interjected here that all fishermen ought to realize that the moment of danger is just when you let down your line. That is the moment when the fish will put up all kinds of games on you, such as rushing at you in a compact mass so fast that you can't take them in, or selecting the largest of their number to snatch away one of your rods.

"We had hardly let down our lines," says the fishermen,—"when Tom got a perfect monster. That fish would have weighed five pounds,— wouldn't it, Tom."——

"Easily," says Tom.

"Well, Tom started to haul him in and he yelled to Ted and me to get the landing net ready and we had him right up to the boat, right up to the very boat," "Right up to the very boat," repeat Tom and Edward sadly. "When the damn line broke and biff! away he went. Say! he must have been two feet long, easily two feet!"

"Did you see him?" asks the young lady who is staying with them. This of course she has no right to ask. It's not a fair question. Among people who go fishing it is ruled out. You may ask if a fish pulled hard, and how much it weighed but you must not ask whether anybody *saw* the fish.

"We could see where he was," says Tom.

Then they go on up to the house carrying the "string" or "catch" and all three saying at intervals,— "Say! if we had only landed that big fellow!"

By the time this anecdote has ripened for winter use, the fish will have been drawn actually into the boat (thus settling all question of seeing it) and will there have knocked Edward senseless, and then leaped over the gunwale.

II

STORY OF THE EXTRAORDINARY BAIT

This is a more advanced form of fishing story. It is told by fisherman for fishermen. It is the sort of thing they relate to one another when fishing out of a motor boat on a lake, when there has been a slight pause in their activity and when the fish for a little while,—say for two hours, have stopped biting. So the fishermen talk and discuss the ways and means of their craft. Somebody says that grasshoppers make good bait: and somebody else asks whether any of them have ever tried Lake Erie soft shell crabs as bait, and then one,—whoever is lucky enough to get in first,—tells the good old bait story.

"The queerest bait I ever saw used," he says, shifting his pipe to the other side of his mouth, "was one day when I was fishing up in one of the lakes back in Maine. We'd got to the spot and got all ready when we suddenly discovered that we'd forgotten the bait,——"

At this point any one of the listeners is entitled by custom to put in the old joke about not forgetting the whiskey,——

"Well there was no use going ashore. We couldn't have got any worms. It was too early for frogs, and it was ten miles to row back home. We tried chunks of meat from our lunch, but nothing doing! Well, then, just for fun I cut a white bone button off my pants and put it on the hook. Say! you ought to have seen those fish go for it. We caught, oh, easily twenty, yes thirty,—in about half an hour. We only quit after we'd cut off all our buttons and our pants were falling off us! Say, hold on boys, I believe I've got a nibble! Sit steady!"

Getting a nibble of course will set up an excitement in any fishing party that puts an end to all story telling. After they have got straight again and the nibble has turned out to be "the bottom" as all nibbles are,—the moment would be fitting for anyone of them to tell the famous story called:

III

BEGINNER'S LUCK, OR THE WONDERFUL CATCH MADE BY THE NARRATORS WIFE'S LADY FRIEND

"Talking of that big catch that you made with the pants button," says another of the anglers, who really means that he is going to talk of something else,—"reminds me of a queer thing I saw myself. We'd gone out fishing for pickerel, 'dorés,' they call them up there in the lake of

Two Mountains. We had a couple of big row boats and we'd taken my wife and the ladies along,—I think there were eight of us, or nine perhaps. Anyway it doesn't matter. Well, there was a young lady there from Dayton, Ohio, and she'd never fished before. In fact she'd never been in a boat before. I don't believe she'd ever been near the water before."

All experienced listeners know now what is coming. They realize the geographical position of Dayton, Ohio, far from the water and shut in everywhere by land. Any prudent fish would make a sneak for shelter if he knew that a young lady from Dayton, Ohio, was after him.

"Well, this girl got an idea that she'd like to fish and we'd rigged up a line for her, just tied on to a cedar pole that we'd cut in the bush. Do you know you'd hardly believe that that girl had hardly got her line into the water when she got a monster. We yelled to her to play it or she'd lose it, but she just heaved it up into the air and right into the boat. She caught seventeen, or twenty-seven, I forget which, one after the other, while the rest of us got nothing. And the fun of it was she didn't know anything about fishing; she

166

just threw the fish up into the air and into the boat. Next day we got her a decent rod with a reel and gave her a lesson or two and then she didn't catch any."

I may say with truth that I have heard this particular story told not only about a girl from Dayton, Ohio, but about a girl from Kansas, a young lady just out from England, about a girl fresh from Paris, and about another girl, not fresh,—the daughter of a minister. In fact if I wished to make sure of a real catch, I would select a girl fresh from Paris or New York and cut off some of my buttons, or hers, and start to fish.

IV

THE STORY OF WHAT WAS FOUND IN THE FISH

The stories however do not end with the mere catching of the fish. There is another familiar line of anecdote that comes in when the fish are to be cleaned and cooked. The fishermen have landed on the rocky shore beside the rushing waterfall and are cleaning their fish to cook them for the midday meal. There is an obstinate superstition that fish cooked thus taste better than first class kippered herring put up in a tin in Aberdeen where they know how. They don't, but it is an honourable fiction and reflects credit on humanity. What is more, all the fishing party compete eagerly for the job of cutting the inside out of the dead fish. In a restaurant they are content to leave that to anybody sunk low enough and unhappy enough to have to do it. But in the woods they fight for the job.

So it happens that presently one of the workers holds up some filthy specimen of something in his hand and says "Look at that! See what I took out of the trout! Unless I mistake it is part of a deer's ear. The deer must have stooped over the stream to drink and the trout bit his ear off."

At which somebody says,—whoever gets it in first,—says.

"It's amazing what you find in fish. I remember once trolling for trout, the big trout, up in Lake Simcoe and just off Eight Mile Point we caught a regular whopper. We had no scales but he weighed easily twenty pounds. We cut him open on the shore afterwards, and say, would you believe it, that fish had inside him a brass buckle,—the whole of it,—and part of a tennis shoe, and a rain check from a baseball game, and seventy-five cents in change. It seems hard to account for it, unless perhaps he'd been swimming round some summer hotel."

These stories, I repeat, may now be properly narrated in the summer fishing season. But of course, as all fishermen know, the true time to tell them is round the winter fire, with a glass of something warm within easy reach, at a time when statements cannot be checked, when weights and measures must not be challenged and when fish grow to their full size and their true beauty. It is such stories as these, whether told in summer or in winter, that the immemorial craft of the angler owes something of its continued charm.

———

HAVE WE GOT THE YEAR BACK-WARDS? IS NOT AUTUMN SPRING?

Once a year with unfailing regularity there comes round a season known as Autumn. For a good many hundred years the poets have been busy with this season as they have with all the others. Around each of them they have created a legend. And the legends are mostly untrue and need correcting.

For example, in spring there is supposed to be a tremendous gayety let loose. The young lamb is said to skip and play; and the young man's fancy is supposed to turn towards thoughts of love. Anybody who has seen a young lamb humped up and shivering in the April rain for want of an overcoat knows just how false this lamb idea is; and anybody who has seen a young man of today getting smoothed up for a winter evening party knows just when the real season of the lovers comes.

There are hawthorns in blossom in the lanes in the spring, and in the winter there are rubber trees in the restaurants with no blossoms at all. But the rubber tree sees more of love in one evening than the hawthorn does in its whole life.

The same kind of myth has gathered round the summer. The poets have described it as rich, luscious, glorious, crowned with flowers and drowsy with the hum of the bee. In reality, summer is the dead time. It is the time of the

sweltering heat and the breathless nights, when
people sleep upside down with their feet on the
rail of the bed; when there is no one in the city
but the farmers and no one on the farms but the
city people; in short when life is all disturbed,
deranged, and out of sorts; when it is too hot to
think, too late to begin anything, and too early to
start something; when intellect dies, oratory is
dumb, and national problems slumber. At such
a time there is nothing of current interest except
the expeditions to the North Pole and the rescue
parties sent out to drag away the explorers.

Then comes autumn. The poet describes it
as the decline of the year. The leaf withers.
The russet woods shiver in the moaning wind.
The poet on his lonely autumn walk talks with
the shepherd on the mutability of life and all is
sadness.

Now it occurs to me all this stuff about Autumn,
as applied here and now, is nonsense. No doubt
it was all true when men lived in woods and
caves, shivered in the rain, and counted the days
until the return of the sun. But in our own time
the thing doesn't fit at all. Autumn is the real
beginning of the year, the new start after the

dead season. Witness, in illustration, some of the glad signs that mark the oncoming of the Autumn season.

THE RETURN OF THE OYSTER. I can imagine no more pleasing sight to the true lover of nature than the first oyster peeping out of its half shell. How dainty is its coloring! How softly it seems to lie upon its little dish! All through the dull, dead summer it has been asleep in its bed of mud, but now Nature has burst forth again and the oyster is back with us.

THE YOUNG LAMB. And alongside of the oyster, look who is here too! The lamb, not the poor ungainly thing that humped up itself in the springtime in a feeble attempt to jump, but the true lamb, valued at a dollar a portion, and eaten along with autumn cauliflowers, Jerusalem artichokes, and October asparagus. With what eager eyes is it regarded by the people who have spent the summer in the country where there are no fresh meat and no vegetables. For the true aspect of the bounty of Nature, give me every time the sight of a butcher shop in autumn, with the pink lobsters nestling in the white celery, pure as snow. When the poet wanted inspiration he went and talked with a shepherd. I'd rather talk with a chef.

And the flowers! Ah, there now is something worth seeing. Look at these autumn chrysanthemums right out of the hothouses, and the gladioluses, or the gladiolalula—if that is the right plural. Even the beautiful big blue violets will soon be with us, at five dollars a bunch.

And no wonder we need the flowers, for with autumn the glad season of happiness is beginning again. Witness as the principal sign of it——

THE RE-OPENING OF THE VAUDE-VILLE SEASON

All through the dull dead summer we have not seen a single "act." We were away from town, or it was too hot, or the theatres in our vicinity were closed.

But now we are all back in our seats again watching The Seven Sisters—can they really be sisters—pounding out music from wine glasses, from sticks of wood, from cowbells—from anything they have handy. Here are again the two wonderful trapeze performers who hurl themselves through the air. So far we have never seen them break their necks. But, courage, a new season is beginning.

Here is the Magician with his cards, and the Strong Man with his dumbbells, and the Trained Dog that actually sits on a stool. They are all back with us again for the opening of another happy season.

The only trouble is to find time to go to see them. So many things are starting up into life all at once in this glad moment of the year. Not only Vaudeville is beginning but Football has opened up again. Here we are crowded into the stadiums—or rather, the stadiora—in tens of thousands, covered with college colors and chrysanthemums, in the bright autumn sunshine, with splendid seats only a quarter of a mile from the game.

Football having started means, of course, that the colleges are all reopening and when that happens we can feel our intellectual life that has been dormant in the dead heat of summer, come back again with a throb. Soon we shall be going again to popular lectures on Social Dynamics, and Intellectual Hydraulics—the kind of thing that

174

brings learning right to the people and leaves it there.

And not only the colleges. The clubs—culture and brotherhood clubs—are all beginning a new season. There are the men's luncheon and speaking clubs and the Ladies Fortnightly, and the Morning Musical, all starting in at once. All through the summer we have never heard a single address. Now in one week we can hear a talk on *Mexican Folk Music,* or on *Two Weeks in Mongolia,* or *Ten Years in Sing Sing.*

The new life is on the move. The dead leaves have been swept up and burnt. The trees no longer spoil the view. The motoring is fine. If the poet on his Autumn walk, sunk in reverie, gets in the way, let him look out or we'll sink him where he'll never come back.

Autumn, crowned with its wreath of celery and lobsters, is with us again!

OUR SUMMER CONVENTION

As Described by One of its Members

Our summer convention,—the first annual convention of Peanut Men,—has just been concluded and has been such a success that I feel I'd like to set down a little account of it in print.

The way it began was that a few of us,—all peanut men—got talking together about every other business except ours having conventions and ours not being represented in this way at all. Everybody knows there are now conventions of the electrical men and the pulp and paper men, and even of professors and psychologists and chiropodists. And as everybody knows, too, these conventions are not merely for business and social purposes, but they are educative as well. People who go to a convention and listen to the papers that are read will learn things about their own business that they never would have thought of.

Anyway, we got together and formed an association and elected officers,—a Grandmaster of the Nuts, and a Grand Kernel, and seven Chief Shucks and a lot of lesser ones,—and decided to hold a convention. We ·restricted the membership,—because that is always found best in conventions,—and made it open only to sellers, roasters, buyers, importers and consumers of peanuts. Others might come as friends but they couldn't appear as Nuts. To make the thing social it was agreed that members might bring their wives, as many as they liked.

We thought first of New York or Chicago as the place for us, but they always seemed too crowded. Then we thought of Montreal and a whole lot of members were all for it, partly because of the beautiful summer climate. But our final choice was Lake Owatawetness in the mountains.

It was a great sight the day we opened up the convention. We had flags across the street and big streamers with *Welcome to the Nuts* and things like that on them and all the delegates rode in open hacks and pinned on each was a big badge with the words *I Am a Complete Nut.* Underneath this motto was his name and his town and his height and weight and his religion and his age.

Well, we all went to the town hall and we had an address of welcome from the Grand Master. They said that it was one of the best addresses ever heard in the town hall and lasted just over two hours. Personally I can't speak for it because I slipped out of the hall a little after it began. I had an idea that I would just ease off a little the first morning and wait till the afternoon to begin the real educative stuff in earnest. There were two other fellows who slipped out about the same time that I did and so we went down to the lake and decided we'd hire a boat and go down the lake fishing so as to be ready for the solid work of the afternoon. One of the fellows was from Wichita, Kansas, and was a Presbyterian and weighed 168 pounds, and the other was from Owen Sound, Ontario, not classified, and weighed 178 pounds and was five feet, nine and a half inches high.

We took some lunch with us so as not to need to get back till two, when the first big conference opened. We had a printed program with us and it showed that at the two o'clock session there was to be a paper read on *The Application of Thermodynamics to the Roasting of Peanuts* and we all agreed that we wouldn't miss it for anything.

Well, we went clear down the lake to where we understood the best fishing was and it was a longer row than we thought. We didn't really start fishing till noon,—not counting one or two spots where we just fished for twenty minutes or so to see if any fish were there but there weren't. After we got to the right place we didn't get a bite at all, which made us want to stay on a while, though it was getting near the time to go back, because it seemed a shame to quit before the fish began to bite, and we were just thinking of leaving when a Methodist from Oshkosh, Wisconsin, who was nearby, caught a black bass, a real peach. There seemed to be a good many other boats coming down, too, and quite near us there was a Catholic delegate from Syracuse (five feet, eight inches) who caught a catfish and two Episcopalians (150 pounds each) from Burlington, Vermont, who seemed to be getting bites all the time.

So we decided to stay. We didn't get so many fish but we all agreed that an afternoon on the water for health's sake was a fine thing to put a man into shape for the convention work. We knew that in the evening Professor Pip of the State Agricultural College was to read a paper on *The Embryology of the Nut* and we wanted to be right on deck for that.

Rowing back just before supper time some one

of us happened to mention cards, just casually, and the delegate from Owen Sound who was un-classified asked me if I ever played poker. I told him that *I had* played it, once or twice, not so much for any money that might be on it, but just for the game itself, as you might say. The man from Wichita said that he had played it that way, too, and that if you took it like that it was a fine game: in fact for a quiet evening's amuse-ment there was nothing like it. We all three agreed that if it hadn't been for wanting to hear Professor's Pip talk on the Embryology of the Peanut we could have had a quiet little game, a three handed game, or, perhaps, get in one or two of the other boys after supper in one of the rooms.

Anyway, after supper we went upstairs and began throwing down hands just to see what would turn up while we were waiting for the lec-ture time and first thing we knew we got seated round the table and started playing and it seemed a pity to quit and go to the lecture. For my part I didn't care so much because I am not so much interested in The Embryology of the Nut as in the selling of it.

Later on I saw a delegate (from Saskatoon, Saskatchewan, a Universal Christian, six feet high) who said that he had spoken with a man who had heard the lecture and that it was fine. It appears there was only a small turn-out, smaller even than in the afternoon, but those who were there and stayed,—some couldn't stay, —said that it was all right. They said it was too long,—a lecture is apt to be too long, and that the professor spoke pretty low, in fact you couldn't exactly hear him, and that you couldn't understand the subject matter but the lecture itself was good. It was all right.

By the next morning we had the convention pretty well in full swing and you could see that the crowd were getting to know one another. This second morning was to be the big morning of the convention because the state governor was to give us an address and everybody felt that it was a great honor to have him come. They had put up a sort of arch for him to drive under, with a motto *Welcome You Big Nut*. They say the governor was awfully pleased with it and still more when they made him a Chief Grand Nut at the morning ceremony.

I didn't hear his address myself, not more than a few sentences. I couldn't stay. He had just begun a survey of the history of the development of the arable land of the state (he had it all in his hand and was reading it) when I had to go. I had said something to some of the boys the night before about golf,—and it appeared that the privileges of the Watawetness Golf Club had been extended to us,—and I felt that I mustn't go back on it. It was disappointing, but there was no use worrying over it.

They said the governor's address was great. It was too long, everybody admitted, and a few took exception to it because it was not exactly connected with the convention, and some criticized it because it was the same address that he had given to the Skiers and Snowshoemen Convention last February. But still it was good.

Playing golf cut me clean out of the afternoon session, too, as I didn't get back till it must have been started. In this session the programme was to divide the convention up into little groups for intensive study of the peanuts, organized by Miss Mutt of the Botany Section of the State Teachers Association. Each study group was to take some topic under a special speaker and exhaust it. But quite a lot of the delegates had gone fishing, and some were playing pool and some were scattered round. It seems they couldn't make up the groups except just the speaker in each group and Miss Mutt herself of course. So Miss Mutt gave them a talk on the Botany of Selling Peanuts. They said it was fine. It was too long, they thought, and would have been much better, ever so much better, if it had been shorter,—quite short; but it was good.

That night was the big banquet. The governor stayed over for it, and there was to be his speech and the Secretary of Agriculture and speeches from the Grand Master, and from Clergymen, and Teachers. In fact it looked pretty good and from all I heard it was considered a big success. The only thing against it was that some of the delegates had brought in some stuff into the hotel (I don't know where they got it from), and a lot of them were slipping out of the banquet room and slipping up to the rooms where they had this stuff.

Some didn't come down. They said quite a lot didn't come down. I went up there for a while but I didn't stay long, or not so very long, and when I got back to the door of the banquet room, one of the guests, a minister, was talking on the moral aspect of Importing Peanuts. So I didn't stay, as I am 'more interested in the selling aspect.

The next morning I left early. There was to be another whole day and some mighty interesting papers to be read. But I felt I would be needed badly in my business at this time; in fact I felt pretty keen to get back to it. I saw many other delegates come away on the same train, a lot of them. They had taken off their badges, so I couldn't tell their names and their religions but they all agreed that the convention had been a wonderful success and a great educative influence in our business.

V
TRAVEL AND MOVEMENT

All Aboard for Europe

Some Humble Advice for Travellers

EVERY summer thousands and thousands of our people in America go across to Europe. They say that about fifty thousand people leave on the steamers every week. It's either fifty thousand or five hundred thousand, or five thousand—I forget which. Anyway, there are a great many people travelling every year.

Some of them go because they need a change of air; some to improve their minds; some because they were tired of making money, and others because they were tired of not making money. And some again go to see Europe, before it all falls to pieces: and others go just simply and plainly for a vacation because they want for a few weeks to be really happy.

It is especially for this last class that these

few words of advice are written. If you want
to be happy when you start off on a sea voyage
you have got to be prepared to face a lot of disillusionment. You are going to find all through
the trip the most striking difference between
travel as it is pictured in the Guide Book and
travel as it is in fact.

The difference begins at the very moment of
embarkation. Here is what is said in the attrac-
tive Steamship Guide Book—done up in colors
with a picture of two girls walking on a prome-
nade deck, and swaying in the wind like rushes,
while a young man goes past in flannels and a
straw hat.

"What," asks the Guide Book, "is more delightful than the embarkation on an Atlantic
voyage? The size of the great steamer, its spotless decks, its commodious cabins, its luxurious
saloon and its cozy library, thrill us with a sense
of pleasure to come. As we step on board and
look about us at the dancing waters of the harbor
ruffled under the breeze from the open sea beyond, we feel that now at least we are entering
on the realization of our dreams."

188

Yes. Exactly. Only unfortunately, my dear reader, it is just at the very moment of embarkation that you are certain to discover that your black valise is missing. Your steamer trunk is there all right in your stateroom and the brown valise and the paper parcel that your aunt has asked you to deliver in Aberdeen when you land at Liverpool. But the black valise apparently is clean gone.

You certainly had it in the Pullman car and your sister remembers seeing it in the taxicab— but where is it? Talk about embarkation on the ruffled harbor and the unrealized dream! Who can think of these things with a valise missing and the huge whistle of the steamer booming out the time of departure?

No use asking that man in uniform; apparently he's only one of the officers. Don't try to fight your way up to the bridge and challenge the captain. He doesn't know. Round the purser there are twenty people in the same condition as yourself, over one thing or another, all trying to get at him and bite him. There seem to be lots of stewards running up and down, but all they can do is to ask you what number is your stateroom and say that the valise ought to be there. A conspiracy, evidently, the whole thing.

The result is that you are fussing up and down for a half an hour and when at last the valise is found (in the next stateroom, owing to the simple fact that you wrote the wrong number on it), you are already far out at sea and have never seen the embarkation at all.

Never mind, there's lots of the trip left yet. After all, listen to what the Guide Book says about our first morning at sea——

"There is an extraordinary exhilaration," it prattles on, "about the first day at sea. From the lofty deck of the great liner our eye sweeps the limitless expanse. All about is the blue of the Atlantic, ruffled with the zephyrs of a summer morning. We walk the deck with a sense of resilience, a fullness of life unknown to the dweller upon terra firma, or stand gazing in dreamy reverie at the eternal ocean."

Oh, we do, do we? But I guess not. On our first morning at sea we have too much else to think of, even in the calmest weather, than mere reverie on the ocean. What is troubling us, is

the question of deck chairs,—how do we get one?
—are they free, or do we have to pay?—and if
we pay now, do we have to tip the man?—and
which man is it that gives out our chairs?—and
if we want to get our chairs next to Mr. Snyder
from Pittsburgh, whom do we see about it?

There is room enough in this problem to keep
us busy all morning; and even when we have got
it straight, we start all over again with the question of what do we do to get the seat that we want
at the table. We would like to get ourselves and
Mr. Snyder and Mr. and Mrs. Hopkins from
Alberta all at the same table. Somebody has
said to somebody that there's a steward giving
out seats or going to give out seats somewhere
in one of the saloons or somewhere. That's
enough for us. That keeps us hot and busy all
morning.

And you will find, alas my dear reader, that no
matter what the Guide Book says about it, that
kind of worry is going to haunt you all the way.
When you have done with the valises and the deck
chairs and the seats at the table you still have
plenty of other problems to fret over, such
as,——

The English customs officers,—What do they do? Do they examine everything? Will they say anything about those canvas slippers that your aunt has asked you to deliver to her cousin in Nottingham (close to London)? If you explain that she made the slippers, does that make any difference? Or, at any rate, can you say to the man, "Oh very well, I'll send them back to America rather than pay a cent on them?" In short, the English customs officers—what do they do? Travelers lie awake at night and think of that.

And along with that——

At what hour will you land at Liverpool and will you be able to get the 11.30 train to London or will you have to wait for the 12.30? That's an excellent one. Many travelers have thought so hard about that and talked so much about it on deck, that they never even noticed the blue of the sea, and the rush of the flying fish or the great dolphins that flopped up beside the ship.

But even allowing that you can perhaps get a train—some train—from Liverpool, more intense worries set in as we near the other side.

The question of letters, telegrams and mar-

conigrams.   When the purser says that he has
no messages for you and no letters for you, is
he not perhaps getting your name wrong.   He
may have made a mistake.   Might it not be better to go to him again (the fourth time) and ask
him whether he got your name quite right?   By
all means, and let Mr. Snyder go too, and you can
both stand in line at the purser's window and fret
it out together and thus never see the Norwegian
sailing ship under full canvas two hundred yards
away.

But there is worse yet——

The ocean is crossed the trials are over and
the land is in sight.   And again the little Guide
Book breaks out in ingenuous joy!

"Land in sight!   With what a thrill we go
forward to the front of the ship and look ahead
to catch a glimpse of the white cliffs of old England rising from the sea.   All the romance of
history and of exploration rises to the mind with
this first view of the old land.   We stand gazing forward, as might have stood a Columbus
or a Cabot filled with the mystery of the New
Land."

Do we?   No, we don't.   We've no time for

it. As a matter of fact, we don't get any such first glimpse at all. We are down below, wrestling with the problem of how much we ought to tip the bath room steward. Is eight shillings what he gets, or is six enough? We feel we need information, light, knowledge. We must try to find Mr. Snyder and learn what he thinks the bathroom steward ought to get.

And then, somehow, before we know it, and while we are still worrying and fretting over stewards and tips and baggage, our voyage is all over—the time is gone—and we are saying goodbye to the passengers and Mr. Snyder and Mr. and Mrs. Hopkins of Alberta, and the stewards and the purser—noble fellows they all seem now. But we have a queer sense of loss and disillusionment as if our voyage had not yet begun, and a strange longing that we might have it all over again and this time know enough not to spoil it with our poor meaningless worries.

My friend, this is a parable. As is the Atlantic voyage, so is our little pilgrimage in life, a brief transit in the sunshine from shore to shore, whose short days are all too often marred by the mean disputes and the poor worries that in the end signify nothing. While there is still time, let us look about us to the horizon.

———

THE GASOLINE GOODBYE

And What Would Have Happened to the Big Moments of History If the Motor Had Taken a Hand in Them

In the days before the motor car, when a man said goodbye he shook hands and he was gone. If he was to ride on horseback, he made a brief farewell to each person present, shook hands, leaped upon his horse and was off.

Now that the motor car has come into use as the general instrument of visiting, this no longer happens. The people say goodbye, get into their motor car, and are *not* gone. They make an affectionate farewell and then sit looking out of their glass windows, while the car goes "Phut, phut—bang,"—and sticks there.

The more dramatic the goodbye, the more

195

touching the farewell, the more determined the car always is to say "Phut, phut—bang," and refuse to move.

Witness the familiar scene of the goodbye of the Joneses to the Smiths at 6 P. M. on any Sunday evening at any rural place where city people spend their vacation. The Joneses have motored over in their own car—a real peach, tin all over —and have spent Sunday afternoon with the Smiths, who have a cottage for the summer which they call OPEN HOUSE, and where they take care that nobody gets in at meal times.

When the time has come for the Joneses to go, they all mingle up in a group with the Smiths and everybody says goodbye to everybody else, and shakes hands with each one, and they all say, "Well, we certainly had a grand time." Then they all climb into the car with Mr. Jones himself at the wheel and they put their heads out of the windows and they say, "Well, goodbye, goodbye!" and wave their hands.

And then the car goes:——

"Whr-r-r-r-r-r-r-r-r-r-r-r—phut, bang!"

A wisp of thin blue smoke rolls away and when it has gone the Joneses are seen sitting there, absolutely still. The car hasn't moved an inch.

Jones at the wheel sticks his head down among the grips and clutches and says— "I guess she is a little cold," and the Smiths say— "Yes, it often takes a little time to start them." Then there's a pause and nothing seems to be happening and then very suddenly and cheerfully the engine of the car starts making a loud——

"Pur-r-r-r-r-r-r-r-r-r-r-r-r-r-r-r !"

On this, all the Joneses and all the Smiths break out into goodbyes again. All talking together:

"Well, come back soon— We certainly will— We sure had a great time— Remember us all to Alf— We certainly will— You certainly have a nice cottage here— We certainly enjoyed that lemonade—well—goodbye, goodbye, goodbye !"

And then the car goes,——

"Whir-r-r-r-r-r-r-r-r-r-r-r—phut, bang !"

And there is another biff of blue smoke, and when it clears away, what is behind it? Why, the Joneses, right there in their car.

When the machine goes "bang !" all the Joneses

in the car and all the Smiths standing beside the road are knocked into silence for a few seconds. Then Jones mutters— "Seems to be something wrong with the ignition"—and somebody else says— "She doesn't seem to be feeding right"— and there's a little chorus of—"Oh, she is just a little cold, they take a little warming up"— she'll start in a minute."

And then again the machine begins, this time at a terrific speed, about a million revolutions to the minute——

"Whir-r-r-r-r-r-r-r-r-r-r-r-r-r-r-r-r-r-r-r-r-r-r-r-r-R-R-!"

At this happy sound the goodbyes break out all over again in a chorus.

"Goodbye— Look after yourselves— Tell Min we'll see her Friday—goodbye— We certainly had a——"

"Bang!"

All stopped again.

This time Jones is determined that when the engine starts he'll keep it started. There shall be no false alarms this time. "Let her get going good," some of them advise him. And so when the engine next starts Jones doesn't throw in his clutch but just lets her go on humming and roaring till everybody feels assured that this time the start is actually going to happen and the goodbyes erupt all over again.

The noise gets louder and louder, the conversation rises into shouts mixed with the "phut, phut, phut" of the machine, and then all of a sudden there's a tremendous "bang!" and a volume of blue smoke and when it clears away—where are the Joneses?

Gone—clean gone, they seem to have vanished off the earth! At last you catch a glimpse of their car already two hundred yards away, disappearing in a cloud of smoke.

"They're off!" murmur the Smiths, and the painful scene is over . . .

Thinking over all this, I cannot but reflect how fortunate it has been for mankind that the motor car was not invented earlier in our history. So many of the great dramas of history have turned upon farewells and departures that some of the most romantic pages of the past would have been spoiled if there had been any gasoline in them.

Take for example the familiar case of Napoleon saying goodbye to his officers and soldiers at Fountainebleau before going to exile. The fallen emperor stood beside the steed he was about to mount, turned a moment and addressed to his devoted comrades words that still echo in the ears of France. But suppose that he had said the same thing while seated in a little one-seater car with his head stuck out of the window. How inadequate it would have sounded:——

"Farewell, my brave comrades—phut, phut—together we shared the labor and the burden of a hundred campaigns—phut, bang, phut—we must forget that we have conquered Europe—whir-r-r, phut—that our eagles have flown over every capital—bang—I leave you now for exile, but my heart forever will remain—whir-r-r, phut—buried in the soil of France, bang!"

Or take as a similar case in point the famous farewell to the nation spoken by George Washington as his last service to the republic that he had created.

General Washington, supposing there had been gasoline in those days, would have been reported as leaning out from the window of his sedan car and speaking as follows:——

"Let America cultivate and preserve the friendship of the world—phut, phut—let us have peace and friendship with all—whir-r-r—and entangling alliances with none—bang! I have grown old in the service of this country and there is something wrong with my ignition. To each and all of you I bid now a last farewell——

"Whir-r-r-r—

"Farewell!

"Phut, phut, phut, phut.

"Farewell!

"Bang!"

COMPLETE GUIDE AND HISTORY OF THE SOUTH

Based on the Best Models of Traveler's Impressions——

In setting down here my impression of southern life, southern character, southern industry, and what I am led to call the soul of the southern people, I am compelled to admit that these impressions are necessarily incomplete. The time at my disposal—twenty-four hours less fifteen minutes while I was shaving—was, as I myself felt, inadequate for the purpose.

I could have spent double, nay treble, nay quadruple the time in the South with profit, and could have secured twice, nay three times, nay four times as many impressions. At the same time I may say in apology that my impressions, such as they are, are based on the very best models of travelers' impressions which are published in such floods by visitors to this continent.

To one who has the eye to see it, the journey south from New York to Washington, which may be called the capital of the United States, is filled with interest. The broad farm lands of New Jersey, the view of the city of Philadelphia, and the crossing of the spacious waters of the Susquehanna, offer a picture well worth carrying away. Unfortunately I did not see it. It was night when I went through. But I read about it in the railroad folder next morning.

After passing Washington the traveler finds himself in the country of the Civil War, where the landscape recalls at every turn the great struggle of sixty years ago. Here is the Acquia

Creek and here is Fredericksburg, the scene of one of the most disastrous defeats of the northern armies. I missed it, I am sorry to say. I was eating lunch and didn't see it. But the porter told me that we had passed Fredericksburg.

It is however with a certain thrill that one finds oneself passing Richmond, the home of the Lost Cause, were there still lingers all the romance of the glory that once was. Unluckily our train didn't go by Richmond but straight south via Lynchburg Junction. But if it had I might have seen it.

As one continues the journey southward, one realizes that one is in the South. The conviction was gradually borne in on me as I kept going south that I was getting South. It is an impression, I believe, which all travelers have noted in proportion as they proceed south.

I could not help saying to myself, "I am now in the South." It is a feeling I have never had in the North. As I looked from the train window I could not resist remarking, "So this is the South." I have every reason to believe that it was.

One becomes conscious of a difference of life,

of atmosphere, of the character of the people. The typical southerner is courteous, chivalrous, with an old-world air about him. I noted that on asking one of my fellow travelers for a match he responded, "I am deeply sorry, I fear I have none. I had a match in my other pants yesterday, but I left them at home. Perhaps I could go back and get them."

Another gentleman in the smoking room of whom I ventured to ask the time replied, "I am deeply sorry, I have no watch. But if you will wait till we get to the next station, I will get out and buy a clock and let you know." I thanked him, but thought it the part of good taste to refuse his offer.

Every day one hears everywhere reminiscences and talk of the Civil War. Nearly everybody with whom I fell into conversation—and I kept falling into it—had something to say or to recall about the days of Lee and Jackson and of what I may call the Southern Confederacy.

One old gentleman told me that he remembered the war as if it were yesterday, having participated in a number of the great episodes of the struggle. He told me that after General Lee had been killed at Gettysburg, Andrew Jackson was almost in despair; and yet had the Southerners only known it, there was at the time only a thin screen of two hundred thousand union troops between them and Washington.

In the light of these conversations and reminiscences it was interesting presently to find oneself in Georgia and to realize that one was traversing the ground of Sherman's famous march to the sea. Unluckily for me, it was night when we went through, but I knew where we were because during a temporary stoppage of the train, I put my head out of the curtains and said to the porter, "Where are we?" and he answered "Georgia." As I looked out into the profound darkness that enveloped us, I realized as never before the difficulty of Sherman's task.

At this point, perhaps it may be well to say something of the women of the South, a topic without which no impression would be worth publishing. The southern women, one finds, are distinguished everywhere by their dignity and reserve. (Two women came into the Pullman car where I was, and when I offered one of them an apple she wouldn't take it.) But they possess at the same time a charm and graciousness that is all their own. (When I said to the other woman that it was a good deal warmer than it had been she smiled and said that it certainly was.)

The Southern woman is essentially womanly and yet entirely able to look after herself. (These two went right into the dining car by themselves without waiting for me or seeming to want me.) Of the beauty of the Southern type there can be no doubt. (I saw a girl with bobbed-hair on the platform at Danville, but when I waved to her even her hair would not wave.)

On the morning following we found ourselves approaching Birmingham, Alabama. On looking at it out of the car window, I saw at once that Birmingham contains a population of 200,-000 inhabitants, having grown greatly in the last decade; that the town boasts not less than sixteen churches and several large hotels of the modern type.

I saw also that it is rapidly becoming a seat of manufacture, possessing in 1921 not less than 14,000 spindles, while its blast furnaces bid fair to rival those of Pittsburgh, Pennsylvania and Hangkow, China; I noticed that the leading denomination is Methodist, both white and colored, but the Roman Catholic, the Episcopalian and other churches are also represented. The town, as I saw at a glance, enjoys exceptional educational opportunities, the enrollment of pupils in the high schools numbering half a million.

The impression which I carried away from Birmingham enabled me to form some idea (that is all I ever get) of the new economic growth of the South. Everywhere one sees evidence of the fertility of the soil and the relative ease of sustenance. (I saw a man buy a whole bunch of bananas and eat them right in the car.) The growth of wealth is remarkable. (I noticed a man hand out a fifty dollar bill in the dining car and get change as if it were nothing.)

I had originally intended to devote my time after leaving Birmingham to the investigation and analysis of the *soul* of the South, for which I had reserved four hours. Unfortunately I was not able to do so. I got called in to join a poker game in the drawing room and it lasted all the way to New Orleans.

But even in the imperfect form in which I have been able to put together these memoirs of travel I feel on looking over them that they are all right, or at least as good as the sort of stuff that is handed out every month in the magazines.

———

THE GIVE AND TAKE OF TRAVEL

A Study in Petty Larceny, Pro and Con

I have recently noted among my possessions a narrow black comb and a flat brown hairbrush. I imagine they must belong to the Pullman Car Company. As I have three of the Company's brushes and combs already, I shall be glad to hand these back at any time when the company cares to send for them.

I· have also a copy of the New Testament in plain good print which is marked "put here by the Gibbons" and which I believe I got from either the Ritz-Carlton Hotel in Montreal or the Biltmore ·in New York. I do not know any of the Gibbons. But the hotel may have the

208

book at any time, as I have finished with it. I will bring it to them.

On the other hand, I shall be very greatly obliged if the man who has my winter overshoes (left on the Twentieth Century Limited) will let me have them back again. As the winter is soon coming I shall need them. If he will leave them at any agreed spot three miles from a town I will undertake not to prosecute him.

I mention these matters not so much for their own sake as because they form part of the system of give and take which plays a considerable part in my existence.

Like many people who have to travel a great deal I get absent-minded about it. I move to and fro among trains and hotels shepherded by red-caps and escorted by bell boys. I have been in so many hotels that they all look alike. If there is any difference in the faces of the hotel clerks I can't see it. If there is any way of distinguishing one waiter from another I don't know it. There is the same underground barber surrounded by white marble and carrying on the same conversation all the way from Halifax to

Los Angeles. In short I have been in so many
towns that I never know where I am.

Under these circumstances a man of careless
disposition and absent mind easily annexes and
easily loses small items of property. In a Pullman car there is no difficulty whatever, if one
has the disposition for it, in saying to a man sitting beside you, "Good morning, sir. It looks
like a beautiful day," and then reaching over and
packing his hair brush into your valise. If he is
the right kind of man he will never notice it, or
at best he will say in return, "A beautiful morning," and then take away your necktie.

There is, let it be noticed, all the difference in
the world between this process and petty larceny.

The thing I mean couldn't possibly be done by
a thief. He wouldn't have the nerve, the quiet
assurance, the manner. It is the absolute inno-
cence of the thing that does it. For example, if
a man offers me a cigarette I find that I take his
cigarette case and put it in my pocket. When I
rise from my hotel dinner I carry away the nap-
kin. When I leave my hotel room I always take
away the key.

There is no real sense in this: I have more

hotel keys than I can use as it is. But the fault is partly with our hotels. So many of them put up a little notice beside the door that reads, "Have You Forgotten Anything?" When ever I see this I stand in thought a minute and then it occurs to me, "Why of course, the Key!" and I take it with me.

I am aware that there is a class of persons— women mostly—who carry away spoons and other things deliberately as souvenirs. But I disclaim all connection with that kind of thing. That is not what I meant at all.

I would never take a valuable spoon, unless I happened to be using it at the table to open the back of my watch, or something of the sort. But when I sign my name on the hotel book I keep the pen. Similarly and in all fairness, I give up my own fountain pen to the telegraph clerk. The theory works both ways.

As a rule, there is nothing more in all this than a harmless give and take, a sort of profit and loss account to which any traveler easily becomes accustomed. But at the same time one should be careful. The theory may go a little too far. I remember not long ago coming home from a theatre in Trenton, New Jersey, with a lady's white silk scarf about my neck.

I had no notion how it had got there. Whether the woman had carelessly wrapped it about my neck in mistake for her own, or whether I had unwound it off her, I cannot say. But I regret the incident and will gladly put the scarf back on her neck at any time. I will also take this occasion to express my regret for the pair of boots which I put on in a Pullman car in Syracuse in the dark of a winter morning.

There is a special arrangement on the New York Central whereby at Syracuse passengers making connections for the South are allowed to get up at four and dress while the others are still asleep. There are signs put up adjuring everybody to keep as quiet as possible. Naturally, these passengers get the best of everything and, within limits, it is fair enough as they have to get up so early. But the boots of which I speak outclass anything I ever bought for myself and I am sorry about them.

Our American railways have very wisely taken firm grounds on this problem of property mislaid or exchanged or lost on the Pullman cars. As everybody knows when one of our trains reaches a depot the passengers leave it with as mad a haste as if it were full of smallpox. In fact, they are all lined up at the door like cattle in a pen ready to break loose before the train stops. What happens to the car itself afterwards they don't care. It is known only to those who have left a hair brush in the car and tried to find it.

But in reality, the car is instantly rushed off to a siding, its number-placard taken out of the window so that it cannot be distinguished, after which a vacuum cleaner is turned on and sucks up any loose property that is left in it. Meantime the porter has avoided all detection by an instantaneous change of costume in which he appears disguised as a member of the Pittsburgh Yacht Club. If he could be caught at this time his pockets would be found to be full of fountain pens, rings and current magazines.

I do not mean to imply for a moment that our railways are acting in a dishonest way in the matter. On the contrary, they have no intention of keeping or annexing their passengers' property. But very naturally they do not want a lot of random people rummaging through their cars. They endeavor, however, through their central offices to make as fair a division of the lost-and-found property as they can. Anyone applying in the proper way can have some of it. I have always found in this respect the greatest readiness to give me a fair share of everything.

A few months ago for example I had occasion to send to the Canadian National Railway a telegram which read, "Have left gray fedora hat with black band on your Toronto-Chicago train." Within an hour I got back a message, "Your gray fedora hat being sent you from Windsor, Ontario." And a little later on the same day I received another message which read, "Sending gray hat from Chicago," and an hour after that, "Gray hat found at Sheboygan, Michigan."

Indeed, I think I am not exaggerating when I say that any of our great Canadian and American Railways will send you anything of that sort if you telegraph for it. In my own case the theory has become a regular practice. I telegraph to the New York Central, "Please forward me spring overcoat in a light gray or fawn," and they send it immediately; or I call up the Canadian Pacific on the telephone and ask them if they can let me have a pair of tan boots and if possible a suit of golf clothes.

I have found that our leading hotels are even more punctilious in respect to their things than the railways. It is now hardly safe to attempt to leave in their rooms anything that one doesn't want. Last month, having cut my razor strop so badly that it was of no further use, I was foolish enough to leave it hanging in a room in the Biltmore Hotel in New York. On my return home I got a letter which read: "Dear Sir: We beg to inform you that you have left your razor strop in room 2216. We have had your strop packed in excelsior packing and await your instructions in regard to it."

I telegraphed back, "Please keep razor strop. You may have it." After which in due course I got a further letter which said, "We are pleased to inform you that the razor strop which you so generously gave to this Company has been laid before our board of directors who have directed us to express their delight and appreciation at your generous gift. Any time you want a room and bath let us know."

VI
GREAT NATIONAL
PROBLEMS

The Laundry Problem

A Yearning for the Good Old Days of the Humble Washerwoman

A LONG time ago, thirty or forty years ago, there used to exist a humble being called a Washerwoman. It was her simple function to appear at intervals with a huge basket, carry away soiled clothes, and bring them back as snow-white linen.

The washerwoman is gone now. Her place is taken by the Amalgamated Laundry Company. She is gone but I want her back.

The washerwoman, in fact and in fiction, was supposed to represent the bottom end of everything. She could just manage to exist. She was the last word. Now the Amalgamated Laundry Company uses hydro-electric power, has an office like a bank, and delivers its goods out of a huge hearse driven by a chauffeur in livery. But I want that humble woman back.

In the old days any woman deserted and abandoned in the world took in washing. When all else failed there was at least that. Any woman who wanted to show her independent spirit and force of character threatened to take in washing. It was the last resort of a noble mind. In many of the great works of fiction the heroine's mother almost took in washing.

Women whose ancestry went back to the crusades *very nearly*, though never quite, started to wash when the discovery of the missing will saved them from the suds. But nowadays if a woman exclaimed, "What shall I do? I am alone in the world! I will open an Amalgamated Laundry!" —it would not sound the same.

The operation of the old system—as I recall it from the days of forty years ago—was very simple. The washerwoman used to call and take away my shirt and my collar and while she washed them I wore my other shirt and my other collar. When she came back we changed over. She always had one and I had one. In those days any young man in a fair position needed two shirts.

Where the poor washerwoman was hopelessly

simple was that she never destroyed or injured
the shirt. She never even thought to bite a
piece out with her teeth. When she brought it
back it looked softer and better than ever. It
never occurred to her to tear out one of the
sleeves. If she broke out a button in washing,
she humbly sewed it on again.

When she ironed the shirt it never occurred
to the simple soul to burn a brown mark right
across it. The woman lacked imagination. In
other words, modern industrialism was in its infancy.

I have never witnessed at first hand the proc-
esses of a modern incorporated laundry company
using up-to-date machinery. But I can easily con-
struct in my imagination a vision of what is done
when a package of washing is received. The
shirts are first sorted out and taken to an expert
who rapidly sprinkles them with sulphuric acid.

They then go to the coloring room where they
are dipped in a solution of yellow stain. From
this they pass to the machine-gun room where
holes are shot in them and from there by an
automatic carrier to the hydraulic tearing room
where the sleeves are torn out. After that they

are squeezed absolutely flat under enormous pressure which puts them into such a shape that the buttons can all be ripped up at a single scrape by an expert button ripper.

The last process is altogether handwork and accounts, I am informed, for the heavy cost. A good button-ripper with an expert knowledge of the breaking strain of material, easily earns fifty dollars a day. But the work is very exacting, as not a single button is expected to escape his eye. Of late the big laundries are employing new chemical methods, such as mustard gas, tear bombs, and star shells.

Collars, I understand, are treated in the same way, though the process varies a little according as the aim is to produce the Fuzzled Edge Finish or the Split Side Slit. The general idea, of course, in any first class laundry, is to see that no shirt or collar ever comes back twice. If it should happen to do so, it is sent at once to the Final Destruction Department, who put gun cotton under it and blow it into six bits. It is then labelled *"damaged"* and sent home in a special conveyance with an attendant in the morning.

Had the poor washerwoman kept a machine-gun and a little dynamite, she could have made a fortune. But she didn't know it. In the old days a washerwoman washed a shirt for ten twelfths of a cent—or ten cents a dozen pieces. The best laundries, those which deny all admission to their offices and send back their laundry under an armed guard, now charge one dollar to wash a shirt, with a special rate of twelve dollars a dozen.

On the same scale the washerwoman's wages would be multiplied by a hundred and twenty. She really represented in value an income of fifty dollars a year. Had it been known, she could have been incorporated and dividends picked off her like huckleberries.

Now that I think of it, she was worth even more than that. With the modern laundry a shirt may be worn twice, for one day each time. After that it is blown up. And it costs four dollars to buy a new one. In the old days a shirt lasted till a man outgrew it. As a man approached middle life he found, with a certain satisfaction, that he had outgrown his shirt. He had to spend seventy-five cents on a new one, and that one lasted till he was buried in it.

223

Had some poor woman only known enough to pick up one of these shirts and bite the neck out of it, she might have started something really big.

But even when all this has been said there remains more yet. In the old days if you had a complaint to make to the washerwoman you said it to her straight out. She was *there*. And she heard the complaint and sneaked away with tears in her eyes to her humble home where she read the Bible and drank gin.

But now if you have a complaint to make to an Amalgamated Laundry Corporation, you can't find it. There is no use complaining to the chauffeur in livery. He never saw a shirt in his life.

There is no use going to the office. All you find there are groups of lady employees sheltered behind a cast iron grating. They never saw your shirt. Don't ask them. They have their office work and in the evening they take extension lectures on the modern drama. They wouldn't know a shirt if they saw it.

Nor can you write to the company. I speak here of what I know for I have tried to lay a complaint before a laundry company in writing,

and I know the futility of it.   Here is the letter
I wrote:

> To the Board of Directors,
>   The Amalgamated Universal Laundry
>   Company
> Gentlemen:—
> I wish you would try to be a little more careful
> with my shirt.   I mean the pink one.   I think
> you put a little more starch in the neck last time
> than you intended and it all seems stuck together.
>   Very faithfully yours,——

But the only answer I got was a communica-
tion in the following terms:

> Dear Sir,
> Folio 110,615.   Department 0412.   Received
> February 19th 9.26 A. M.   Read March 19,
> 8.23 A. M.   Sent down April 19th 4:01 A.M.
> Sent up May 19th 2 A. M.
> We beg to inform you that your communica-
> tion as above will be laid before the shareholders
> at the next general meeting.   In answering kindly
> indicate folio, department, street, age and occu-

pation. No complaints received under names or in words.

Yours,
Folio 0016.

After that I felt it was hopeless to go on. My only chance for the future is that I may get to know some beautiful rich woman and perhaps her husband will run away and leave her weeping and penniless and drinking gin, and then I will appear in the doorway and will say, "Dry your tears, dear, dear friend; there is prosperity for you yet; you shall wash my shirt."

THE QUESTIONNAIRE NUISANCE

A Plan to Curb Zealous Investigators in Their Thirst for Knowledge

Everybody who manages an office or carries on a profession or teaches in a college, is getting to be familiar with the thing called "questionnaire." It is a sheet of questions or inquiries sent round broadcast and supposed to deal with some kind of social investigation. Some of these questions come direct from the insane asylums, but others purport to come from students, investigators, and social workers. But wherever they come from, they are rapidly developing into a first class national nuisance.

Here for example on my desk is a letter which reads:

"I am a graduate student of the Myopia Woman's College of Agricultural Technology, and I am making a special investigation of the government ownership of cold storage plants. Will you please write me the history of any three governments which you know to possess cold storage plants? Will you also let me have your opinion on coldness, on storage, and on plants?"

Here is another one that came in by the same mail:

"I am a social worker in Nut College, Nutwood on the Hum, and am making out a chart or diagram to show whether the length of the human ear is receding or going right ahead. Will you kindly measure your ears and let me know about their growth? Keep me advised if they start."

Along with these are letters asking me to give

my opinion, with reasons, whether or not elected aldermen are more crooked than aldermen not even fit to be elected; asking where I stand on the short ballot and what I think of prison reform and the union of the Presbyterian churches.

I have come to the conclusion that something decisive has got to be done about these questionnaires; so I have decided in the interests of myself and other sufferers to write out a model answer for one of them and afterwards to let that answer suffice for all the others. Here is the one that I have selected for answering. I didn't make it up. It is the genuine article, as anyone used to these things will recognize at once.

It runs as follows:

"Dear Sir:

"I am an American college student and I have been selected along with Mr. John Q. Beanhead of the class of 1926, of whom you may have heard, to represent the Bohunk Agriculture College in the forthcoming debate against Skidoo Academy. Our subject of debate is to be on the question: Resolved, that the United States should adopt a parliamentary system of government.

Knowing that you have the knowledge of these problems, and trusting that you will be pleased to answer at once, I have selected the following questions which I hope will not take too much of your valuable time to answer:

"1. How does the efficiency of the British government compare with that of the United States?

"2. Do you think the minority has too much power in the United States?

"3. What is your opinion of a democracy?

"4. What is a responsible government?

"5. How would the adoption of the British system affect our Supreme Court?

"I will sincerely appreciate any further suggestions which you may care to make in answer to these questions or concerning any advantage or defect of either system, or any other system.

"Yours truly,

"O. Y. KNOTT."

The answer which I prepared for Mr. Knott reads as follows:

"Dear Sir:

"As soon as I heard from your letter that the big debate is on between Bohunk and Skidoo, I was thrilled with excitement. Can we win it? Can we put enough international energy behind you and Mr. Beanhead (Do I know of him? How *can* you ask it?) to drive the thing through? I want to say at once that in this business you are to regard my own time as absolutely valueless. I may tell you frankly that from now until the big debate is pulled off I purpose to lay aside every other concern in life and devote myself to your service. I couldn't possibly answer your question in any other way.

"So now let me turn to your actual questions. You ask first, 'How does the efficiency of the British government compare with that of the United States?'

"Here is a nice, straightforward, manly question. You won't object if my answer is of rather extended length, and you must not mind if it takes me a week to get it ready for you. I shall not only have to handle a good deal of historical material, but I also propose to cable to Mr. Stanley Baldwin and ask him how the efficiency of his government is standing right now.

"Your next question asks whether the minority has too much power in the United States. Again a wonderfully shrewd inquiry. How *do* you manage to think of these things? Has it too much power? Let me think a little. In order to answer your question, I'm afraid I shall have to read over the history of the United States from the Declaration of Independence.

"You ask next, What is my opinion of a democracy? This I can answer briefly. It is the form of government under which you are permitted to live.

"Your next question is, 'What is a responsible government?' I admit the keenness of the inquiry. It is amazing the way you get to the center of things. But I am not prepared. Give me a month on this, if you possibly can.

"Your last question (for the present) reads 'How would the adoption of the British System affect our Supreme Court?' Here again I can hardly answer without perhaps fatiguing you with details. But I will write to Justice Taft and to Lord Reading and while we are waiting for their answers perhaps you would care to send me along a few more questions. I can be working on them in my spare time."

I had written the above letter and then on second thoughts I decided not to send it. What would be the use? The kind of young man who sends out these questionnaires is quite impervious to satire.

The only thing to do is to try to form a league of grown-up people who refuse to be investigated. I propose to be the first in it. Henceforth I will answer no questions except to the census taker and the income tax man.

If any college girl is investigating the upward trend of mortality among mules or the downward movement of morality among humans, she need not come to me. If any young man is making a chart or diagram or a graph to show the per capita increase of crime let him go to the penitentiary. My door henceforth is closed.

THIS EXPIRING WORLD

I have just been reading in the press the agonizing statement that there are only 4,000,-000,000,000 cords of pulp wood left in the world, and that in another fifty years it will be all gone. After that there will be no pulp. Who it is that is consuming all this pulp, I do not know. I am sure that in my own home, apart from a little at breakfast, we don't use any.

But the main point is that in fifty years it will all be finished. In fifty years from now, where there used to be great forests of pulp-trees reaching to the furthest horizon, there will be nothing but a sweep of bare rolling rocks, lifeless and untenanted, where nothing will be heard except the mournful cry of the waterfowl circling in the empty sky over what was once the forests of North America.

Or no—I forgot. It seems that there will be no waterfowl either. In the very same newspaper I read that the waterfowl of America are disappearing so fast that in another forty years they will be extinct. Parts of the country that only a few years ago were literally black with black duck, teal, ptarmigan, and pemmican now scarcely support one flamingo to the square mile. In another generation the whole continent will have been turned into farms, fields, motor roads, and the motor cars will have penetrated everywhere.

Motor cars, did I say? I fear I am in error there again. In forty years there will be **no** motor cars. Gasoline, it is certain, is running out. Professor Glumb of Midnight, Alaska, has just made a calculation to show that at the rate at which we are using up the world's gasoline, the supply will end in forty years.

He warns us that even now there are only 4,000,000,000,000,000 gallons in sight. There may be just a little more, he thinks, under the Red Sea; he has not been down, but he doubts if there are more than a couple of million billion gallons. In a little time it will be all gone. The motor cars will stand packed in rows and it won't be possible to move them an inch.

And what is worse, it won't be any use trying to substitute coal. There won't be any. It is to run out the year before gasoline. Our reckless use of it all through the nineteenth century has brought us to the point where there are only 10,000,000,000,000 tons left. Assuming that we go on consuming it, even at our present rate, the last clinkers will be raked out of the last furnace in 1964. After that the furnace man will simply draw his salary and sit in the cellar: there won't be a thing for him to do.

At first some of the scientists—such as Profes-

sor Hoopitup of Joy College—were inclined to
think that electricity might take the place of coal
as a source of power, heat, light, and food. But
it appears not. The electricity is nearly all gone.
Already the Chicago drainage canal has lowered
Niagara Falls the tenth of an inch, and in places
where there was once the white foaming cataract
leaping in a sheet of water a foot thick, there is
now only eleven inches and nine tenths.

We may perhaps last on a little longer if we
dam the St. Lawrence, and dam the drainage
canal, and dam the Hudson—in short, if we dam
the whole continent up and down. But the end
is in sight. In another forty years the last kilo-
watt of electricity will have been consumed, and
the electric apparatus will be put in a museum,
and exhibited as a relic of the past to the children
of the future.

Children? No, no, I forgot. It is hardly
likely there will be any, forty years hence. The
children are disappearing as rapidly as the
gasoline and the waterfowl. It is estimated that
the increase of the birth rate on this continent is
steadily falling. A few years ago it was 40 per
thousand, then it sank to 20, then it passed to

10, and now it is down to decimal four something. If this means anything it means that today we have an average of a thousand adults to decimal four something of a child. The human race on this continent is coming to a full stop.

Moreover, the same fate that is happening to gasoline and coal seems to be overtaking the things of the mind. It is, for example, a subject of universal remark that statesmen seem to be dying out. There may be a few very old statesmen still staggering round, but as a class they are done. In the same way there are no orators: they're gone. And everybody knows that there is hardly such a thing left now as a gentleman of the old school. I think that one was seen a month or so ago somewhere in a marsh in Virginia. But that's about the last. In short, civility is dead, polite culture is gone, and manners are almost extinct.

On the other side of the account I can find nothing conspicuous except the very notable increase of the criminal class. It has recently been calculated by Professor Crook (graduate of Harvard and Sing Sing) that within forty years every other man will belong to the criminal class; and even the man who isn't the other man will be pretty tough himself.

In other words, the outlook is bad. As I see it, there is nothing for it but to enjoy ourselves while we can. The wise man will go out, while it is still possible, and get some pulp and a pint of gasoline and a chunk of coal and have a big time.

ARE WE FASCINATED WITH CRIME?

Most readers will agree with me that of late the newspapers have been fine reading. First there was the account of the new murder in Cleveland where the body was sent away by express. Then there was the story of the bob-haired bandit,—it didn't say whether man or woman,—held up an entire subway station and got clean away with the iron ticket office. There was the man who killed his mother-in-law and refused to give any reason, and the high-school girl of fifteen who shot the teacher because he tried to teach her algebra. Along with this there were two kidnappings, three disappearances of reputable citizens, two degeneracies and a little sprinkling of bank robberies and train wrecking in Arkansas. Take it all in all it made the morning paper well worth reading. With a sheet of news like that the trip on the street car to one's work passes like a moment.

There were of course the foreign murders, too. But I generally keep them for my lunch hour. I find it hard to get up the same interest when they murder Turks and Finns and Letts as when you have the thing right at home. One body packed in a trunk at Cleveland and sent by express is better to me than a whole car-load lot of Letts. I get more out of it. But taking them all together and adding up the home and foreign crimes I found that yesterday's paper was thirty per cent straight criminality. That I think is about a record and will compare very favorably with Soviet Russia or with the Dark Ages. Indeed I doubt if the Dark Ages, even in equatorial Africa, had anything on us in point of interest in crime.

My first feeling over this record was one of pride. But afterwards on reflection I began to feel a little bit disturbed about it, and to wonder whether as a race and a generation we are not getting morbidly fascinated with crime, and liable to suffer for it?

Our newspapers are filled with bandits, safe breakers, home wreckers, crooks, policemen and penitentiaries. The stories that sell best are stories in which there is murder right straight off on the first page. The sneaking fascination of the daring criminal has put the soldier and the patriot nowhere. Stories of brave men who give their lives for their country are now written only for children. Grown up people read about daring criminals, who talk worse English than the first year class at a college and call a trust company a "crib" and a bank manager a "stiff." That is the kind of literature that is making Shakespeare and Milton and Emerson sound like a lecture on anthropology.

If a rich man is killed by his chauffeur in Tampa, Florida, and his body hidden in the gasoline tank, why should you and I worry? We don't live in Tampa and we have no chauffeur and gasoline is too expensive for us to waste like that.

Yet a whole continent will have to sit up and

read a column of news about such a simple little event as that.

I suppose that in a sense this hideous interest in crime and its punishment is as old as humanity. It must have created quite a stir when Cain killed Abel. On our own continent our oldest knowledge of manners and customs is the story of the Indian's delight in torture, feebly paralleled by the Puritan's pleasure in throwing rotten eggs at a sinner in the stocks. In what are now called the "good old times" in England, say about the time of the Tudors, people used to tramp long distances with a "lunch" in their pockets to go and see a man burnt in a sheet of white flame. One reads stories of people taking little children to executions and holding them up to see. Even when the days of the burning were over people still gathered in crowds of a morning round Newgate jail in London to see the hangings. Rare sport it must have been. For a specially good show they were there the night before, sitting up all night to hold the good places.

In what we call the civilized countries mankind has forbidden itself the pleasure of inflicting tortures and watching executions. But we are breaking out in a new spot. The same evil instinct finds another vent. Since we are not allowed any longer to go to executions and to take a personal part in crimes we like to read about them. And the vast apparatus of our press and our telegraph can give us opportunities in this direction of which our ancestors never dreamed. Think what could have been made by a first class New York newspaper organization, and by the moving picture people, of the burning of Latimer and Ridley? It seems like a lost opportunity.

Under our conditions we don't have to confine ourselves, as the man of two centuries ago did, to the crimes of our own neighbourhood. We can gather them in from all the world. He had to be content with a hanging every now and then. We can have a dozen or two every day, and if we care to count Finns and Letts, easily a hundred.

But the moralist,—that's me,—is bound to ask where is it leading us? What is the result of it on our minds and characters, this everlasting dwelling on crime. Somebody wrote long ago that,——

Vice is a monster of such hideous mien,
That to be hated needs but to be seen,
But too oft seen, familiar with her face
We first endure, then pity, then embrace.

The same is true of crime. The everlasting
depiction and perusal of it corrupts the mind,—
not yours of course, my dear reader, because you
are so strong minded. But it corrupts the feeble
mind. Personally I admit that I found myself
reflecting on that man who killed his mother-in-
law and gave no reason and wondering perhaps,—but let it go.

Everybody knows that this North American
Continent,—the people of the United States, the
Canadians, the Mexicans and the Eskimos,—
is undergoing a wave of crime such as was never
known before. Some people attribute this to one
thing, some to another. Some say it is because
of the decline of Presbyterianism, and some say
it is an effect of motor cars. But my own idea
is that the chief cause of it is crime literature,
crime news and universal outbreak of crime interest.

One naturally asks what are we going to do
about it? Many people would immediately sug-

gest that the first thing to be done is to amend
the federal constitution of the United States so
as to forbid all morbid interest in crime; and
then to pass a series of state statutes for hanging anybody who takes too much interest in hanging.

I don't think that the evil can be cured that way.
That is a method of doing things that has worn
pretty thin. In the United States and Canada
we have got so many prohibitive and preventive
statutes already that we are in danger of all
being in jail before we are done with it. The
only remedy is the slow but efficacious force of
public opinion, of what used to be called, in days
before legislatures made statutes, the working
of the spirit.

For social evils the first remedy is a social
consciousness of the evil. If the community becomes conscious of its unwholesome morbid interest in crime, that already will start the cure.
Sensible persons here and there will begin to take
the mote,—or the motor,—out of their own
eye,—as a first step toward taking the beam out
of their neighbors. Newspapers and magazine
makers and moving picture makers have no in-

nate desire to foist crime news on the public. They are probably sick of it. Left to themselves they would rather go fishing or dig in the garden. The notion that a newspaper reporter is half brother to the criminal is erroneous. In point of news, and amusements and pictures, the public always gets what the public wants. This is a pity but it is so.

There is no need for anybody to start a "national movement" in this matter. Personally I refuse to join in it. I have been dragged into too many already,—swatting flies, and going to see mother on May 11th, and never spitting except at home,—my time is all taken up with them.

But anybody can start a movement by beginning with himself. That's what I mean to do. Henceforth it is no use for a newspaper editor to hand me out stories of crime and violence. I'm done with them. I want to read the quiet stuff,—about how the autumn hoe crop is looking, and about the latest lectures on paleontology and how cold it has turned at Nome in Alaska. That kind of thing improves the human mind and does nothing but good.

. . . .

But before I do start, I'd just like to have one little peep at that news I see in today's paper about the man who murdered the barber in Evansville because he was too slow in shaving him. That sounds good, but after that I'm done.

VII
ROUND OUR CITY

At The Ladies Culture Club

A Lecture on The Fourth Dimension

IT has become a fixed understanding that with each approaching winter there begins the open season for the various Ladies Culture Clubs. I suppose that this kind of club exists in everybody else's town just as it does in mine. We have one in my town that meets at eleven (every other Tuesday), has just a small cup of coffee and just a tiny sandwich, hears an hour's talk, usually on music or art, and then goes home.

Then there's one that meets at lunch, every second Thursday and every third Tuesday, quite informally, just eats a tiny beefsteak with a nice dish of apple pie after it and listens to a speech on national affairs, excluding of course all reference to political parties or politics, or public opinion, and all references to actual individuals or actual facts.

After that there's a club, mostly of older women, which meets at three (without refreshments till after) and discusses social problems such as how to keep younger women in hand. This club meets every first Monday in the month unless it falls at the beginning of a week.

But the club that has most interested me recently is the Ladies Culture Club because I had the honor of visiting it a little while ago. The club was founded two winters ago,—as was explained to me over the ice cream by the president—with the idea that it is a pity that women know so little of science and that nowadays science is really becoming a quite important thing, and when you think of radio and electrons and atoms and things like that one ought to know something about them for fear of your feeling ignorant.

So when the club was founded it was made absolutely and exclusively a woman's club, men taking no part in it whatever, except that men are invited to be the speakers and to sit on the platform and attend the meetings.

The day I was there the meeting was held in the ballroom of the new Grand Palaver hotel, because that is a simple place suitable for science. There were no decorations except flowers and no music except a Hungarian orchestra which stopped the moment the lecture began. This is a rule of the club.

The attendance was so large that several of the ladies remarked with pride that it would hardly have been possible to get an equal number of men to come at three o'clock in the afternoon to listen to a lecture on Four Dimensional Space.

. . . .

The great mass of members were seated in chairs on the floor of the ballroom with a certain number of men here and there among them; but they were a peculiar kind of men. The president and a group of ladies were on a raised platform and they had in the middle of them Professor Droon who was to lecture on Four Dimensional Space. In front of him they had put a little table with a glass and water, enough water to last a camel for a four days' trip. Behind Professor Droon was a barricade of chairs and plants with spikes. He couldn't escape.

The president rose and made the regulation announcement that there were a good many members who had not yet paid their fees this season and it was desirable that they should do so owing to the high cost of bringing lecturers to the club.

She then picked up a piece of paper and read from it as follows:

"The Pythagorean philosophers as well as Philolans and Hicetus of Syracuse conceived of space as immaterial. The Alexandrine geometers substituted a conception of rigid co-ordinates which has dominated all scientific thinking until our own day. I will now introduce Professor Droon who will address the members on Four Dimensional Space if the ladies near the doorway will kindly occupy the chairs which are still empty at the front."

Professor Droon, rising behind the water jug, requested the audience in a low voice to dismiss from their minds all preconceived notions of the spatial content of the universe. When they had done this, he asked them in a whisper to disregard the familiar postulate in regard to parallel lines. Indeed, it would be far better, he mur-

mured, if they dismissed all thought of lines as such and substituted the idea of motion through a series of loci conceived as instantaneous in time.

After this he drank half the water and started.

In the address which followed and which lasted for one hour and forty minutes, it was clear that the audience were held in rapt attention. They never removed their eyes from the lecturer's face and remained soundless except that there was a certain amount of interested whispering each time he drank water.

When he mentioned that Euclid, the geometrician, was married four times there were distinct signs of amusement. There was a sigh of commiseration when he said that Archimedes was killed by a Roman soldier just as he was solving a problem in mechanics. And when he mentioned the name of Christopher Columbus there was obvious and general satisfaction.

In fact, the audience followed the lecture word for word. And when at length the professor asked in a whisper whether we could any longer maintain the conception of a discrete universe absolute in time and drank the rest of the water and sat down, the audience knew that it was the end of the lecture and there was a distinct wave of applause.

The comments of the audience as they flowed out of the hall showed how interested they had been. I heard one lady remark that Professor Droon had what she would call a sympathetic face; another said, yes, except that his ears stuck out too far.

Another said that she had heard that he was a very difficult man to live with; and another said that she imagined that all scientists must be because she had a friend who knew a lady who had lived in the same house all one winter with the Marconis and very often Marconi wouldn't eat. There was a good deal of comment on the way the professor's tie was up near his ear and a general feeling that he probably needed looking after.

There was a notice at the door where we went out which said that the next lecture would be by Professor Floyd of the college department of botany on The Morphology of Gymnosperms. They say there will be a big attendance again.

OUR OWN BUSINESS BAROMETER

For Use in Stock Exchanges and Stock Yards

Recently, with the assistance of a group of experts, I have been going into the statistical forecast business.

I have been led to do this by noticing how popular this kind of thing has come to be. All over the country there are banks and trust companies, and statistical bureaus and college departments that send out surveys of business conditions and prophecies of what good business is going to do. In any good high school the senior commercial class are prepared to work out a chart showing what "world conditions" are going to be next month.

I note that this kind of literature is having a wonderful popularity. Many people are so busy nowadays that they have hardly time to read even the latest crime news, such as how the bob-eared bandit held up the Grand Central Station and got away with the entire Information Stand. But they can always find a few leisure moments for

255

reading about the probable effect of the failure of the Siamese rice crop on the motor car industry.

In other words, this kind of literature has come to stay. There is henceforth a regular demand for a wide-eyed, clear-sighted survey of the business field. It is for this reason that I have been led to go into it and with the aid of experts am prepared to offer for the use of business men a brief survey of the prospects of the globe for next month.

We decided, naturally, to begin with the discussion of export wheat. It is the custom of all survey makers to start with the wheat situation and we follow their example. We find that advices from Argentine, from Turkestan and from Simcoe County, Ontario, indicate that the wheat situation is easier than it was. My experts place the Russian output at about half a billion poods while the Egyptian crop is not likely to fall below two hundred million quids. Add to this a Chinese autumn production of at least a million chunks and a first impression is one of exuberance if not hilarity.

But other factors are less reassuring.

There is a visible supply of 10,000,000 bushels of wheat in the elevators at the head of the Great Lakes and 10,000,000 bushels in transit to Liverpool, but on the other hand the Japanese consumption of wheat bread has fallen 3.6 per cent. in the last month and the Chinese will hardly touch it.

Disturbed political conditions in the Argentine republic may result in the cessation of Argentine export but on the other hand improved conditions in Soviet Russia may result in the liberation of the Russian supply. The wheat crop in Hindoostan is said to be in serious danger of destruction from rust but as against that the wheat crop in Persia looks great. Speculative buying on the European exchanges may force the price up but on the other hand speculative selling may force it down. Our expert opinion therefore is that we don't know. Wheat may go up in price; but it may not.

General business conditions, in our opinion, show distinct signs of improvement but they also show unmistakable signs of getting worse. There were 2,100 business failures reported last month in the United States and Canada. But in a way that's nothing. There are a great many people who deserve to fail. Bank deposits, however, increased from \$21,161,482,936.84 to \$22,668,931,056.48, or something like that; we are speaking only from memory.

Sterling exchange in New York opened for the month at \$4.84, rose sharply to \$4.84 $^{26}\!/\!_{32}$, reacted to \$4.83 and then moved steadily up to \$4.89. Why it did this we have been unable to find out.

Meantime the Brazilian revolution has focussed financial attention on the milreis. As far as we can understand what the milreis did, it seems to have risen upwards, fallen down, lain flat, tried to get up, failed, raised itself again and then flopped. Our experts are not prepared to give any opinion as to what the milreis will do next. Some people think this is a good time to buy it, but if it was ours we should sell it. We wouldn't want it round the place.

The movement of prices has been in various directions, some up, some down and some sideways. There was a five per cent. drop in Portland cement, and a ten per cent. fall in pig iron. But we ourselves are not using any just now and were more affected by the rise of 2 cents a gallon in gasoline which hit us hard and shortened our investigations by about ten miles a day.

During the same period under consideration there have been strikes, lockouts, earthquakes, cloudbursts, insurrections and other disturbing conditions beyond even the power of a senior commercial class to calculate.

Taking all these factors into consideration our conclusion upon the whole is that we don't know what business is going to do next month, and we don't believe that anyone else does. It is our humble opinion that a problem which contains among its factors the weather, earthquakes, snowstorms, revolutions, insurrections, labor, the tariff, the wishes and desires of one and three quarter billions of human beings and the legislation of over a thousand legislatures is a little beyond us.

We will go a little further. We incline to believe, and our experts agree with us (they are paid to), that all this business barometer, statistical forecast stuff means nothing more than the age-long desire of the human race for prophecies. There is no doubt people like to listen to a good prophecy. Children have their fortunes read in the leaves of tea-cups. Servant girls pay a quarter to have a negress do it with a pack of cards. And cultivated people pay five dollars to get a divination from a Persian astrologer hailing from East Thirteenth Street, New York.

And so the business man has started up his own particular form of divination in his new statistical forecast. Our advice to our business clients (as we do not propose to stay in the forecast business) is this. If you want a really good forecast don't bother with all the statistics and the index numbers and the averages. Go and get your fortune told in the good old-fashioned way in words of this sort:

"There is a fair woman coming into your life and there is also a dark woman. One of them will bring you great happiness but beware of the other. You are going to strike a great opportunity of getting rich; but you are also in danger of getting poor. You have nerve but you lack confidence, but if you will cherish your belief in yourself you will never know what a boob you really are. One dollar."

That is the kind of forecast that has been going since the days of the Pharaohs and is still the best known.   Stick to it.

———

MY PINK SUIT

A Study in the New Fashions for Men

This morning I put on my pink suit for the first time, and I must say it looked too cute for anything.   I felt of course that it was an innovation and a great change, but I was glad to be in it.

I suppose everybody has been reading all about the new fashions for men and how over in London and in Paris all the men are wearing suits of pink and sky blue and chrome yellow.   All the London and Paris papers that I have seen say that the new suits are a great success and that the idea is all the rage.   But, as I say, everybody knows about that and I don't need to explain it.   I only wanted to talk about my own suit.

I had it made out of pink georgette undershot with a deep magenta and crossed with an invisible slate blue so that the material shimmers in

261

the light with different colors, and when I walk
up and down in front of a long mirror (I bought
the mirror at the same time as the suit), the
colors run up and down my back in ripples of
moving light. The magenta color seems to suit
my figure, though several of my very best friends
say that personally they think that they prefer
the slate.

I had two or three men over in the morning
to sit up in my room and watch me walk up and
down in front of the glass. Of course, ordi-
narily at that time of the day they would be at
their business, but I just telephoned over to them
and told them that my new suit was such a dar-
ling that they simply *must* come over and see it.
So they came over and we just sat around while
I put on one part of the suit after another and
showed it off in the long glass.

They all agreed that the color was just lovely
and they said they were just crazy to get a suit
like mine. One said that he thought that for
himself the color might be a little young and that
for his age he would rather have a bottle green
or a peacock blue—something a little older, but
I told him that I was quite sure he could wear

262

anything just as young as anybody. In fact, I know a man who is past sixty, who can wear pink for evening wear, and who looks just as young in it as anybody else would.

Perhaps I should explain, as I know a lot of my friends would like to know about it, just how I had my suit cut. The coat is made rather full at the chest and then brought in at the waist line and cut out again very full about the hips with gores and with ruffled insertions of pleated chiffon at the point where the back falls to the hips.

It has a ruching round the neck and is wattled around the collar with an accordion frill brought round just below the ears and then thrown back so as to show the back of the neck. Some of my friends thought that instead of a ruching they would rather have had a little frill of lace so cut as to show the throat. But I doubt whether, with my throat, this would be so good.

The buttons are in a large size of mother-of-pearl and are carried in a bold line edgeways from the shoulder to the waist with two more buttons larger still, behind at the place where the back dips in above the hips.

Everybody agreed that the buttons are very

bold, but they thought that they would be quieter on the street than in the house.

The waistcoat is cut very simply and snugly so as to show the curve of the stomach as far as possible. It has just one little pink bow at the bottom, but beyond that it is quite plain. One or two of my friends thought that it might be a little too severe, but most of us agreed that though it might seem severe indoors it wouldn't be so at all out of doors, especially on high ground.

The trousers are cut very snug around the line of the hips with gored insertion at each side so as to give free play for leaping or jumping and then are flared out to the knee where they are quite full and wide. They end, absolutely, only a little way below the knee and of course they need to be worn over clocked stockings or else I have to have my legs tattooed. They seem terribly short when I put them on, but everybody says that it is the length they are wearing in Paris and in London and that some of the men are even cutting off their trousers half way between the waistcoat and the knee.

I must say that I felt a little strange in my

pink suit when I went out presently on the street in it. One of the men asked me to lunch with him, so I went out in my suit with just a little straw hat, half size, and a bunch of violets in the lapel of my coat. I felt quite shy at first and quite different from my usual self, and I think I even blushed when some one came across to my table at lunch and told me he had never seen me look so well.

I went over to my office in the afternoon and the very first person who came in to do business with me said he was delighted with my suit, and so we sat and talked about it for a long time and he told me of an awfully good shirtmaker that he could recommend if I wanted to get some of the shirts they are wearing. He said that over in London they are all going in for fancy shirts to match the new suits and that the colors they wear are the most daring you can imagine. He told me that a friend of his, quite an elderly man, had just got back from the other side wearing a canary-colored shirt with pussy willow tassels round his neck, and that it was really quite becoming.

Other people came into my office later in the day and we did nothing but talk about the new styles and how delicious it is going to be for men to dress in all the colors they like to wear.

On my way home in the street car which was rather crowded, a man got up and gave me his seat, and of course I thanked him with a smile that showed all my teeth, but I didn't speak to him because I wasn't sure whether I ought to speak to strangers, in my pink suit.

Well, when I got home I first stood and looked at myself in the long glass for quite a while. And then—I don't know just why—I went and took off my new pink costume and put on the old gray suit that I had worn the day before. It was made, as far as I remember, about two and a half, or else four and a half, years ago.

It has no ruching, crocheting, or insertions in it, and it isn't flared or gored or pleated, and it doesn't sweep boldly round the hips or the neck or anywhere. It has a bulge here and there where I have sat on it or knelt in it or hung it on the electric light. The pockets of it stick out a good deal from having been filled up with pipes and tins of tobacco and fishing tackle. There is more or less ink on it, but nothing that really injures it for use.

Somehow I think I'll go back to it.

WHY I LEFT OUR SOCIAL WORKERS GUILD

We recently started in our town,—as I suppose most people would have started in most towns,—an organization called the Social Workers Guild. Our idea was that we would try to do good in the community around us. We would send children from the slums down to the sea, and bring children up from the sea to go to college. Wherever we find a poor widow living in a basement with a string of children and a new baby appearing every year, we would turn up on the threshold with a great basketful of toys. If a plumber was out of work and nearly in despair, just then one of our agents would drop a broken furnace in his lap. Anybody who has ever felt the fascination of that kind of thing, knows just what I mean.

And the best of it all was that all the cost of

doing good was to be met by the proceeds of entertainments and amusements organized by the Guild, so that really we gave our money without knowing it and had all the fun thrown in.

I don't want to say a single word against the general idea of such Social Guilds as ours. They are certainly very noble in intention. But as I have been led to terminate absolutely and for ever my own membership of the Guild, I will explain the reason for my doing so by publishing my correspondence with Mr. J. Brazil Nut, the secretary of the league, or rather the series of letters sent by Mr. Brazil Nut to me.

LETTER NO. I

Dear Sir,

I beg to inform you that the Committee of the Guild has discovered a very distressing case of a family who came here from Cyprus two years ago and are anxious to return home but are unable to do so. At the present time they are living in a small apartment of which we need only say that not a single window faces the south, that there is no elevator although the place is three stories high, and that the condition of the front steps is deplorable and the door bell apparently *permanently out of order*. The landlord, we regret to say, stubbornly refuses to knock the place down.

The father of the family is a good workman and only too willing to work. His trade is that of a camel driver and hitherto he has been unable to find a camel. But he says that if money could be found he would go back to Cyprus where he knows of a camel.

Our Committee considering the case a deserving one, has decided to hold a dance in the Social Guild Workers Hall on Saturday evening next. It is proposed to engage Bimbasti's orchestra and, in view of the distressing nature of the case, to serve a light supper for which tables may be reserved by telephone. The price of the tickets, of which I am venturing to send you two, will be $10.00 each, the ticket carrying with it the privilige of eating supper, or of leaving without eating it, as may be preferred.

Yours very faithfully,

J. Brazil Nut

Secretary of the S. W. G.

LETTER NO. 2.

Dear Sir,

I have much pleasure in thanking you for your very generous subscription for two tickets for the dance and supper given last week by the Guild in aid of a distressed family from Cyprus, and in informing you that the affair was organized and carried through with great success and with great enjoyment by all concerned. Some fifty couples participated in the dancing, and the whole, or at least seventy five per cent., of the supper was eaten on the spot.

Unfortunately the expenses of the affair proved more heavy than was expected. Taking into account the fee for Bimbasti's orchestra and the cost of bunting, flowers and supper, our Committee is faced with a deficit of about five hundred dollars. Some of the ladies of the Committee have proposed that we give this entire deficit to the family from Cyprus, or perhaps try to buy them a camel with it.

But the general feeling is in favor of carrying the deficit forward and wiping it out by an in-

formal vaudeville entertainment to be held in the
Hall of the Guild next Saturday evening. In
view of the high cost of the talent to be engaged
we have decided to place the tickets at $25.00 or
three for $100.00. I am venturing to send you
five, which you are at entire liberty to keep, and
send me the money, or, if you prefer to do so,
you may return the tickets with the money.

Meantime I regret to say that our field committee has reported one or two more very distressing cases. We have on our hands the case
of a man, a master mechanic, by trade a maker
of blow torches, who appears hopelessly addicted
to drink. The man himself confesses that he is
quite unable to get along without alcohol. Our
workers find it extremely difficult, under present
conditions, to get him any. But they think, and
the man himself agrees, that if they could give
this man a sea trip to South America he would
need no alcohol at least until his return. Our
Committee are also anxious to obtain funds to
buy a wooden leg, for a professional beggar who
needs it in his business. It seems that he has in-
advertently lost the leg he had. A week ago

after his work he put his leg into his valise and carried it home as usual. But there in some way it disappeared.

It is now proposed that all these cases shall be collectively disposed of by our special vaudeville entertainment, and I trust that you will undertake to take at least five tickets.

Very faithfully,

J. Brazil Nut

Secretary of the S. W. G.

LETTER NO. 3

Dear Sir,

In thanking you for your very generous subscription for five tickets for the Guild Vaudeville entertainment of last Saturday which you were not able to attend, I desire to inform you that the performance was an unqualified success. Although slightly delayed in starting and not beginning until a quarter to eleven and briefly interrupted later on by the going out of the electric lights for half an hour, the whole affair was most enjoyable. The amateur performance of our treasurer Mr. Jones with the dumb-bells,—quite as heavy as anything seen on the stage,—was voted extraordinary and the Social Guild Girls Christian Chorus might have been mistaken for regular music hall work.

Unfortunately the paid numbers cost us heavily and out of all proportion to our receipts. I regret to say that we are face to face with a deficit of some two thousand dollars.

In order to avoid the heavy personal assessment represented by this sum, our committee now proposes to hold, three weeks from to-day, an indoor Kermesse or Bazaar to last for three days. It is suggested that we engage the armories building and have the floor divided up into booths with little streets in between, with a restaurant and dance floor. The Kermesse will undertake the sale of a great variety of goods which will be purchased in advance by funds advanced by various members of the Guild who have been elected Patrons and Associate Patrons. It is understood that any Associate Patron may advance $1,000, receiving it back out of the profits, while a Patron has the privilege of advancing $2,000. I am glad to inform you also that you have been elected unanimously to be a patron.

Our needs of the profits of this Kermesse are all the greater in so much as the cases reported by our field workers increase in numbers and in gravity. We have before us the case of a family from Honolulu who have recently arrived here and are sorry that they came. They think they would like to go to Tugugigalpa in Honduras,— either there or Winnipeg. We have also a skilled mechanic, very deserving, whose trade was making eye-pieces for the periscopes of German submarines and who is unable to find work.

But we look confidently to the success of our forthcoming Kermesse to put everything on a new footing.

Very faithfully yours,
J. Brazil Nut.

LETTER NO. 4

Dear Sir,

In writing to inform you of the disastrous failure of the Kermesse, held by this Guild, for which your name was put down as a Patron, we feel it only proper to say that the failure was due to no lack of interest or enthusiasm on the part of our members. The careful revision of our accounts by experts seems to show that the financial failure arose very largely from the fact that the articles disposed of were sold at a much lower price than what was paid for them. Some of our best experts agree that this would involve a loss of money. But others note that we lost money also from the fact that we had to pay for rent, for heat, for light as well as for illumination and warmth.

But all agree that there need have been no loss if the premises had been bigger, the restaurant larger, the music louder, the crowds greater and the deficit heavier. I am now laying before our committee a plan for holding a Winter Festival which is to last one month. It will be held in one of the larger hotels, the entire building being taken over for our purpose. We shall also take over one of the railway stations and probably one of the abattoirs and two or three of the larger provision houses.

As before we are nominating patrons who are entitled to underwrite, or subscribe, or guarantee,

any sum over $50,000 which they feel disposed
to offer.   All such sum will be paid back on the
last day of the festival.

Yours very faithfully,
J. Brazil Nut.

LETTER NO. 5

*(This time from the Honorary President of
the Society—Mr. Tridout Solidhead, one of our
leading business men.)*

Dear Sir,
In refusing to accept your very generous resignation from the Social Workers Guild, I beg to
inform you that we have decided to suspend for
the present the plan of a winter festival proposed by Mr. Brazil Nut.   Instead of this we
are accepting the resignation of Mr. Nut from
his position of secretary and we are proposing to
give him a gold watch with a chain and padlock
as a mark of our esteem.   The presentation will
be made at a dinner which will be given to Mr.
Nut before he is taken away to where he is going.   I am sure that you will be delighted to

276

subscribe to the dinner (25 cents) and to the cost of the watch (10 cents per member).

Our new committee have looked into some of our urgent field cases and disposed of them. It appears that the family from Cyprus were alluding to Cyprus, Ohio, and we have invited them to walk there. The man from Honolulu we are having taught by a negro to play the Hawaiian ukulele, and we have got for the man with the wooden leg a situation as a timber cruiser with a lumber company.

We have meantime put the question of the back deficit into the hands of a group of business men. They propose to wipe it out by holding a small entertainment at which (by a special license from the municipality) they will operate a roulette table, and a faro bank, with the sale of cold drinks, selected by a business committee, on the side. They are now looking for a suitable place, about twelve feet by fifteen, to hold this entertainment in.

Meantime we trust you will reconsider your resignation. We are having this matter of a public charity looked into by some of our best business men. Already they incline to the idea that

277

if it is carried on in the right spirit and with proper energy and self-sacrifice, there may be money in it.

Very sincerely,
A. Tridout Solidhead.

VIII
THE CHRISTMAS GHOST

The Christmas Ghost

Unemployment in One of our Oldest Industries

THE other night I was sitting up late,—
away after nine o'clock,—thinking about
Christmas because it was getting near at
hand. And, like everybody else who muses on
that subject, I was thinking of the great changes
that have taken place in regard to Christmas. I
was contrasting Christmas in the old country
house of a century ago, with the fires roaring up
the chimneys, and Christmas in the modern apartment on the ninth floor with the gasoline genera-
tor turned on for the maid's bath.

I was thinking of the old stage coach on the
snowy road with its roof piled high with Christmas turkeys and a rosy-faced "guard" blowing on
a keybugle and the passengers getting down every
mile or so at a crooked inn to drink hot spiced

ale,—and I was comparing all that with the upper berth No. 6, car 220, train No. 53.

I was thinking of the Christmas landscape of long ago when night settled down upon it with the twinkle of light from the houses miles apart among the spruce trees, and contrasting the scene with the glare of motor lights upon the highways of today. I was thinking of the lonely highwayman shivering round with his clumsy pistols, and comparing the poor fellow's efforts with the high class bandits of today blowing up a steel express car with nitroglycerine and disappearing in a roar of gasoline explosions.

In other words I was contrasting yesterday and today. And on the whole yesterday seemed all to the good.

Nor was it only the warmth and romance and snugness of the old Christmas that seemed superior to our days, but Christmas carried with it then a special kind of thrill with its queer terrors, its empty heaths, its lonely graveyards, and its house that stood alone in a wood, haunted.

And thinking of that it occurred to me how completely the ghost business seems to be dying out of our Christmas literature. Not so very long ago there couldn't be a decent Christmas story or Christmas adventure without a ghost in it, whereas nowadays,——

And just at that moment I looked and saw that there was a ghost in the room.

I can't imagine how he got in, but there he was, sitting in the other easy chair in the dark corner away from the firelight. He had on my own dressing gown and one saw but little of his face.

"Are you a ghost?" I asked. "Yes," he said, "worse luck, I am."

I noticed as he spoke that he seemed to wave and shiver as if he were made of smoke. I couldn't help but pity the poor fellow, he seemed so immaterial.

"Do you mind," he went on, in the same dejected tone, "if I sit here and haunt you for a while?"

"By all means," I said, "please do."

"Thanks," he answered, "I haven't had anything decent to work on for years and years. This is Christmas eve, isn't it?"

"Yes," I said, "Christmas eve."

"Used to be my busiest night," the ghost complained, "best night of the whole year,—and now,—say," he said, "would you believe it! I went down this evening to that dinner dance they have at the Ritz Carlton and I thought I'd haunt it,—thought I'd stand behind one of the tables as a silent spectre, the way I used to in King George III's time——"

"Well?" I said.

"They put me out!" groaned the ghost, "the head waiter came up to me and said that he didn't allow silent spectres in the dining room. I was put out."

He groaned again.

"You seem," I said, "rather down on your luck?"

"Can you wonder?" said the ghost, and another shiver rippled up and down him. "I can't get anything to do. Talk of the unemployed,— listen!" he went on, speaking with something like animation, "let me tell you the story of my life——"

"Can you make it short?" I said.

"I'll try. A hundred years ago,——"

"Oh, I say!" I protested.

"I committed a terrible crime, a murder on the highway,——"

"You'd get six months for that nowadays," I said.

"I was never detected. An innocent man was hanged. I died but I couldn't rest. I haunted the house beside the highway where the murder had been done. It had happened on Christmas eve, and so, every year on that night,——"

"I know," I interrupted, "you were heard dragging round a chain and moaning and that sort of thing; I've often read about it."

"Precisely," said the ghost, "and for about eighty years it worked out admirably. People became afraid, the house was deserted, trees and shrubs grew thick around it, the wind whistled through its empty chimneys and its broken windows, and at night the lonely wayfarer went shuddering past and heard with terror the sound of a cry scarce human, while a cold sweat——"

"Quite so," I said, "a cold sweat. And what next?"

"The days of the motor car came and they paved the highways and knocked down the house and built a big garage there, with electricity as bright as day. You can't haunt a garage, can you? I tried to stick on and do a little groan-

285

ing, but nobody seemed to pay any attention; and anyway, I got nervous about the gasoline. I'm too immaterial to be round where's there's gasoline. A fellow would blow up, wouldn't he?"

"He might," I said, "so what happened?"

"Well, one day somebody in the garage actually *saw* me and he threw a monkey wrench at me and told me to get to hell out of the garage. So I went."

"And after that?"

"I haunted round; I've kept on haunting round, but it's no good, there's nothing in it. Houses, hotels, I've tried it all. Once I thought that if I couldn't make a hit any other way, at least I could haunt children. You remember how little children used to live in terror of ghosts and see them in the dark corners of their bedrooms? Well, I admit it was a low down thing to do, but I tried that."

"And it didn't work?"

"Work! I should say not. I went one night to a bedroom where a couple of little boys were sleeping and I started in with a few groans and then half materialized myself, so that I could just be seen. One of the kids sat up in bed and

286

nudged the other and said, 'Say! I do believe there's a ghost in the room!' And the other said, 'Hold on; don't scare him. Let's get the radio set and see if it'll go right through him.'

"They both hopped out of bed as brisk as bees and one called downstairs, 'Dad, we've got a ghost up here! We don't know whether he's just an emanation or partially material. We're going to stick radio into him,—' Believe me," continued the ghost, "that was all I waited to hear. Electricity just knocks me edgeways."

He shuddered. Then he went on.

"Well it's been like that ever since,—nowhere to go and nothing to haunt. I've tried all the big hotels, railway stations, everywhere. Once I tried to haunt a Pullman car, but I had hardly started before I observed a notice, *'Quiet is requested for those already retired,'* and I had to quit."

"Well, then," I said, "why don't you just get immaterial or dematerial or whatever you call it, and keep so? Why not go away wherever you belong and stay there?"

"That's the worst of it," answered the ghost, "they won't let us. They haul us back. These spiritualists have learned the trick of it and they just summon us up any time they like. They get a dollar apiece for each materialization, but what do we get?"

The ghost paused and a sort of spasm went all through him. "Gol darn it," he exclaimed, "they're at me now. There's a group of fools somewhere sitting round a table at a Christmas eve party and they're calling up a ghost just for fun,—a darned poor notion of fun, I call it— I'd like to—like to——"

But his voice trailed off, He seemed to collapse as he sat and my dressing gown fell on the floor. And at that moment I heard the ringing of the bells that meant it was Christmas midnight, and I knew that the poor fellow had been dragged off to work.

FINIS